The Essential Guide to English Studies

Peter Childs

continuum

Continuum International Publishing Group
The Tower Building   80 Maiden Lane
11 York Road   Suite 704
London SE1 7NX   New York NY 10038

www.continuumbooks.com

British Library Cataloguing-in-Publication Data
A catalogue record for this book is available from the British Library.

ISBN: 978–0–8264–8818–3 (Hardback)
       978–0–8264–8819–0 (Paperback)

Library of Congress Cataloging-in-Publication Data
A catalog record for this book is available from the Library of Congress.

Typeset by RefineCatch Limited, Bungay, Suffolk
Printed and bound in Great Britain by MPG Books Ltd, Bodmin, Cornwall

Contents

Acknowledgements

A book such as this cannot be written without drawing on the knowledge, expertise, example and experience of others. Thanks are due to Debbie Davis and colleagues in the English Department at the University of Gloucestershire, Ben Knights and the English Subject Centre team, and all the staff and students with whom I have taught and studied English over the last 20 years.

Special thanks go to Claire Philpott who researched and drafted several of the sections of this book while working as a research assistant at the University of Gloucestershire. Debby Thacker and Peter Widdowson helped in the drafting of particular sections of the book through offering advice and examples at various stages of the project's development.

I would finally like to thank the Higher Education Academy for the support provided by the award of a National Teaching Fellowship, without which this book would not have been written.

About the author

Since taking his undergraduate degree (BA), Peter Childs has accumulated 20 years of experience studying and teaching English in a wide range of universities and colleges. He gave up a career in industry in 1989 to study to become an English lecturer after a first degree in economics at an old University and another part-time degree in literature and philosophy with the Open University. Following a Master's (MA) degree and a year spent teaching English in a college of higher education, he gained a Doctorate (PhD) from another old university, where he also taught and has since worked in the post–1992 university sector.

PART ONE: The basics

This book is intended to be of use to all students starting on or contemplating a higher education (HE) course in English. It seeks to be practical and is not simply an introduction to studying at university or to the subject of English, but to both. You will find helpful facts and figures to conceptualize and contextualize your experience in HE, and English in particular, as well as tips on studying, advice on careers, insights into the mechanics of assessment, information on the language of HE, pointers on guides and references to further study. In short, *The Essential Guide to English Studies* aims to be the first stop for all new and prospective English students.

The book is written with the experience of previous and current students informing the comments and observations. So, to begin with, it will be useful to hear from a number of different voices, which range from an individual perspective to opinions expressed through a large national survey. First, one student offers the following initial key points of advice.

Study tips from a graduate of English

Preparing to come to university: once you have a place at a college or university you will probably be sent a reading list from the English Department, which includes all of the essential reading for the first term or semester. You will also be sent information on the processes for registration and induction, which gives details of such things as on-line registration, identification checks, welcome meetings and other induction activities. This information should be read carefully to avoid unnecessary confusion once you arrive at the university.

Student union activities in Freshers' Week: Student unions offer a comprehensive programme of social activities for new students during the initial week(s) at university. The university's website should provide full details of events as well as other relevant information on the Student union, such as sports clubs and societies.

Freshers' Fayres: every university has one or more Freshers' Fayres; these are worth attending both to meet people and to find out what's going on. For example, there may be three Freshers' Fayres at your university: a Commercial Fayre; a Jobshop Fayre; and a Sports and Societies Fayre. The Commercial Fayre hosts companies, such as nightclubs, fitness clubs and shops, which usually give away free promotional gifts to students. A Jobshop Fayre hosts local firms and recruitment companies, all seeking to find part-time employees: providing a good opportunity to find part-time employment. A Sports and Societies Fayre will host a diverse spectrum of groups, which may range from an African Society to a Musical, Acting and Dancing (MAD) group, as well as sports clubs enrolling you for hockey, badminton or gymnastics.

Beginning lectures and seminars: lectures and seminars for your chosen modules usually begin in the first week. It is extremely important to attend these first classes because they will provide you with the essentials of your learning programme as well as the necessary information to pursue your own independent research.

Assignments: at the beginning of each course/unit/module you should be given details of all assessments and the dates on which these will need to be submitted.

Summer vacations: it is well worth getting into the habit of doing the principal reading for the course in the summer vacation before each level; this is vital so that you are prepared when you begin your dissertation or other major independent-study work at level 3.

Time management: make sure you set aside specific times to do reading, research and assignments each week. It is helpful if you can buy a diary to note down what you will be doing and when; alternatively, you could keep lists in a notebook, providing you prioritize the things you have to do. You need to make sure you are both well organized and self-motivated, otherwise your work will suffer.

Understanding: university provides an intellectually challenging environment, so be prepared to find that you may not understand everything. Read books, handouts and essays several times so that you can gain a firm grasp of the ideas being discussed. Use a dictionary and a guide to literary terms. Most importantly, do not be afraid to ask questions of lecturers – they are there to help you learn.

You-time: make sure you do spend some time socializing: either join a society that interests you, or take up a sport, in order to relax. A word of warning, however, although it is good to enjoy yourself, do not allow too much socializing to affect your studies in a negative way.

Tuning in: this is important if you are going to study success-fully. It refers to the ability to engage with a text and understand ideas relating to it, as well as its technical features. Do not worry if you find this a challenge initially; seminars are a good opportunity to get assistance in learning how to study effectively, by sharing ideas and experiences with other students.

Investigate: it is important to research assignments thoroughly in order to gain a firm grasp of what the question is asking. There is a range of resources available in order to help you with this, both within the library and on the internet. But be careful not to depend too much on critical material, as it is more important to develop your own ideas and opinions about a text.

Presentations: you may be asked to do individual or group presentations, which are an excellent opportunity to develop employment skills. Once you have decided upon the focus of your presentation it is important to research the subject thoroughly and practise your presentation before the real thing. The use of a com-puter or overhead projector, as well as the production of handouts, makes a presentation look much more professional. Unless you are giving a seminar paper where the presentational aspects themselves are not a focus, it is not helpful simply to write down everything that you want to say on a sheet of paper and read from it – your presentation will be much more successful if you use prompt cards and expand on the ideas listed on them while presenting. If you are working in a group, make sure you all know what your area will be and organize regular meetings to discuss progress as well as to prac-tise. Finally, make sure you have a thorough grasp of the concepts you will be discussing because it is probable that you will be asked questions at the end.

Seminars and lectures: it is essential that you attend seminars and lectures in order to get the best out of studying English. Make sure you have done the required reading before you attend so that you have some understanding of the texts, subjects and concepts under discussion. Although it can be tempting to take lots of notes in lectures and seminars, it is advisable to keep this to a minimum because you will learn more if you are able to listen to what the lecturer or other students are saying. It is important to try to contribute to seminars, even if you feel intimidated by the situation; remember that the other students are in the same position. Seminars and lectures provide a great opportunity to broaden your understanding of a text, as well as exchange ideas – so do not miss out.

As a second example of helpful student advice, the following questions and answers are the culmination of a survey of existing students on life as an English undergraduate at one university. It will give you some insight into what it is like to be a student as well as answering some of the questions you might like to ask an existing English undergraduate.

Q: What do you like most about studying English at university?

A: The modules available are both interesting and varied, meaning you can choose a programme of study that reflects your existing interests or you can try areas of English that you have not encountered before. Seminar classes provide a good opportunity to discuss texts and authors with fellow students; they are often lively and intellectually stimulating experiences. The authors you study are extremely wide ranging: from Shakespeare to Zadie Smith, from James Joyce to Edward Said. University gives you the chance to learn, expand your thinking and meet other people who appreciate language and literature.

Q: What is the one thing you wish you had known or been told before coming to university?

A: That it is often your responsibility to take the initiative and find things out for yourself: how to make module selections, details about timetables and registration procedures.

Q: What is the chief difficulty with balancing time commitments (study/work/play) at university?

A: Deadlines for assignments may fall close together, which can make it stressful when trying to balance other commitments. Also there is a great deal of reading to do, so you have to be organized in order to prepare properly for seminars.

Q: How is studying at university different from what you had expected?

A: The crucial areas are time management and reading load. There is enough time to get all of the work done – reading, research and assignments – outside of university contact time (see the Glossary at the end of the book), but you have to be disciplined. The hours in which you study can be as flexible as you want to make them, but it is easy to get behind if you do not devote enough time to reading.

Q: What are the most important things to get sorted in the first semester?

A: Make sure you have copies of all the books that you will need; it helps to have read them as early as possible. Practise your time management skills too. On the non-academic side, it is easy for many people to feel isolated and lonely, so make the effort to meet other people and remember that everybody is in the same situation.

Q: What is the best advice that you would give to a new student at level one?

A: Be systematic with assignments so that work does not build up; it will be much less stressful if you set aside time in which to develop them instead of leaving the writing until the last minute. If you are unsure of anything or have problems, then seek advice from the lecturers or another relevant member of staff.

Q: Do you have any other comments to pass on to new students about how best to adjust to the experience of English studies in HE?

A: Join the English Society if there is one. Such organizations run lots of events and they are a great chance to meet like-minded people, not all of who may necessarily be studying English. Although adjusting to university can be difficult initially, depending on your life circumstances, it does get easier, especially if you make the effort to mix. For most people it is a really good experience, both academically and socially.

Q: Finally, what do you like least about studying at university?

A: Financial considerations. You have to be very careful with budgeting, and it may well be a necessity to work part-time while studying to cover living costs. This means that you have to juggle a lot of different commitments.

As indicated here, a matter on which students often want practical advice concerns finances. There are many places you will find this available, but some statistics and a few facts will be helpful. About 40 per cent of students work part-time to help their financial situation. Many student unions advise that you should not work more than 15 hours a week because of the difficulties of coping with both academic and work commitments. Only 30 per cent of students in 2004 expected to leave university with a debt of less than £8000, and this is likely to be increasing year on year. Fifty per cent expected their final debt to be between £8000 and £15 000. Debt also varies with subject studied. Those studying maths or a science subject usually have greater debts than students in the humanities. Around 40 per cent of students said they had less than £40 a week to live on after paying for accommodation, and around a quarter of all students now live at home. Indeed, proximity to the family home is now the most common deciding factor in choosing a university.

The *Times Higher Educational Supplement* published, in April 2004, the results of a survey of 2000 full-time students across 30 universities. Students were asked: 'What is your single biggest concern?'

Their responses were:

- Achieving desired degree classification – 29 per cent.
- Finding a job after graduation – 14 per cent.
- Debt at graduation – 14 per cent.
- Day-to-day financial worries – 19 per cent.
- Balancing academic, work and social commitments – 9 per cent.
- Self-motivation – 6 per cent.
- Heavy university workload – 4 per cent.
- Pressure to succeed due to financial cost of university – 3 per cent.
- Homesickness – 2 per cent.[1]

This range of response reflects the priorities of the wide diversity of people likely to be studying at university or college in the twenty-first century. Government targets in the UK aim for 50 per cent of people under the age of 30 to have had some experience of higher education (HE) from 2010 onwards. Different measures have been introduced to try to achieve this. In March 2007, one initiative was to have all applicants indicate if their parents went to university or college used as a criterion for deciding who to recruit, giving preferential treatment to those whose mother and father had no experience of HE. To meet their targets in the area of access and widening participation (recruiting students from non-traditional backgrounds), universities can also ask applicants about their ethnicity and their parents' education and occupations, under changes agreed by the Universities and Colleges Admissions Service (UCAS). This has been seen as both social engineering and as affirmative action on equal opportunities. Either way, the intention that everyone who can benefit from higher education should do so is a good one and this book is aimed at everyone considering going into higher education to study a branch of English studies.

The government's agenda has not affected all academic subjects in the same way or to the same extent: the emphasis on employability skills has in many ways aligned the agenda more with practical and vocational subjects, which traditionally do not include English studies. This need not be the case, however, and a suite of subjects such as English literature, English language and creative writing is well placed to attract increasing numbers of students who wish both to develop their interest in expression and analysis and also cultivate the knowledge and understanding that will allow them to enter a range of professions with confidence. Among other things, this book is therefore an attempt to contribute to the perception of English studies as a multi-vocational subject that equips people well for life and work. It will thus refer to such things as the English Benchmarking Statement, which has been widely acknowledged as a useful guide to English graduate skills (see Glossary entry on: English 'Subject benchmark statement').

The English Subject Centre (see Glossary) has written a very useful guide on access and widening participation for English studies. It shows the ways in which, through interviews, recruitment and induction procedures, skills training, the Special Educational Needs and Disability Act 2001(SENDA) compliance, support for mature students and carers, curriculum design and information technology (IT) provision, as well as career-planning support, English departments are changing and enhancing their practices to attract and care for students from non-traditional backgrounds. The report received a broad spectrum of insightful and interesting responses when asking students their reasons for 'choosing English'. For students who were returning to education in order to improve their family's prospects, for example, it often appeared that vocational degrees seemed more realistic options than courses in English studies until they did some investigation into the employment prospects of humanities graduates. One student commented that:

> I came through an Access course and all I thought I could do was a vocational degree leading to a career. But I was told [at the English subject meeting on an access open day] to spend the time thinking about who I was and what I wanted. I had felt that I had to do a vocational degree as I have children who need support and the whole point was to find better employment.

Later she reflected:

> I sometimes wonder where I would be heading if I had been doing a business or IT degree. It would have been easier in a way as it would theoretically lead to a job [but] other types of degree don't make you feel something extra in every aspect of your life. English has that capacity and that is the great thrill of it.[2]

1 Higher education

With the growing emphasis on widening access to higher education (HE), it should come as no surprise that higher educations
institutions (HEIs) are increasingly diverse in character and kind. In
2005 there were 116 universities and 53 higher education colleges,
including one privately funded HEI: the University of Buckingham.
Civic red-brick universities were founded in the late nineteenth
and early to mid twentieth centuries, while the 'medieval' universities of Oxford and Cambridge date from the twelfth/
thirteenth centuries. The first Scottish-, Irish- and English-speaking
North American universities date from the fifteenth (St Andrews,
Glasgow and Aberdeen), sixteenth (Dublin) and eighteenth centuries (New Brunswick). Many 'old' universities were founded in the
1950s and 1960s, when they were known as 'new universities' – a
title they lost with the subsequent creation of a new sector of universities in the 1990s. This was when the former polytechnics, often
called new universities even though most of them have long and
varied roots as institutions, were given university status under the
Further and Higher Education Act of 1992. These universities may
have developed from technical colleges, teacher training colleges or
mechanics institutes, and are likely to be less science-intensive than
older universities and to place more emphasis on their teaching
rather than research excellence. Several colleges of higher education
have additionally been made universities since 1992. Which type of
university or college you would like to go to will probably depend
on such factors as geographical considerations, your preferred mode
of study, and the HEI's specialisms, facilities, reputation and image.
Size varies greatly too, and may affect your choice. The Open University, which largely teaches by distance learning, has over 180 000
students, but the full-time, campus based universities vary from Leeds
Metropolitan, which has over 40 000 students, to the University of

Abertay in Dundee which has fewer than 5000. The average size of HE colleges, which are generally smaller than universities, is 3500 students.

Deciding which kind of institution to go to is therefore a major task, alongside the question of which subject(s) to study. The qualifications that students study for are also diverse and less than half will be studying as a 'standard' student, under 20 years of age and straight from school. About half of students in the UK are first-degree undergraduates, while a quarter are studying for postgraduate certificates or diplomas, Master's and Doctoral (PhD) degrees; a final quarter are studying for an HND (Higher National Diploma), a DipHE (Diploma in Higher Education), or a Foundation Degree. There are over 50 000 different higher education courses in the UK and, from fewer than one million in 1987, there are now well over two million students in the 169 HEIs in the UK. Nearly 90 per cent of that number come from the UK, and about 5 per cent travel from other European countries. The UK spends about 1 per cent of gross domestic product (GDP) on HE, which is similar to most comparable countries except for Australia (1.5%), and Canada, Korea and the USA (at least 2.5%).

Who studies English?

According to figures published by the Higher Education Statistics Agency (HESA), 58 410 students were enrolled on English studies courses in 2004–5. This figure can be further broken down as: 37 735 (full-time undergraduates); 3330 (full-time postgraduates); 14 175 (part-time undergraduates); and 3170 (part-time postgraduates). Another breakdown, for the following year, tells us that 50 325 came from the UK, 2095 from the EU and 12 590 from outside the EU. Of the British students, 36 810 were female and 13 515 were male, emphasizing that the subject is more popular among women. Reassuringly for many people, after the introduction of variable or 'top-up' fees in September 2006 (when home students began to be charged about £3000 per year in fees), the latest figures for 2007 showed that the number of people applying to full-time undergraduate courses in English at UK universities and colleges had increased by 7.6 per cent on the previous year, making

English the fifth highest subject in terms of applicant numbers, after law, psychology, pre-clinical medicine and management.

According to studies, with regard to those undergraduates enrolled for Single Honours English, the number of full-time students on a course ranges from 23 to over 700, with the number of part-time students ranging from 1 to 210. In terms of numbers of full-time students enrolled on a Combined Honours English course, the figures range from 1 to 700, and about half of all undergraduates reading English do so in tandem with studying another subject, as part of Combined Honours or Joint Honours programmes. English is also a central subject in most modular schemes in the humanities, which allow students to choose from a range of different modules or units within an overall suite of humanities subjects (including history, women's studies, English studies, writing, American studies or religious studies).

In respect of ethnicity in HE, of the 673 775 first-year UK undergraduate students in 2004–5, 516 705 were white and 99 290 were from ethnic minorities, which is broken down as: 9,945 (Caribbean descent); 20,315 (African descent); 2,570 (other black background); 19,765 (Indian descent);12,070 (Pakistani descent); 4,440 (Bangladeshi descent); 5,205 (Chinese); 8,125 (other Asian); 16,855 (other, including mixed); the rest were 'unknown'.[1]

In terms of other facets to the student population, fewer than 8 per cent of undergraduate students studying English in 2000 described themselves as disabled. According to staff perceptions, more students in recent years have been coming to their degree course with an English language qualification and more have come from the HEI's local area, although mature students seem to be fewer in number in the twenty-first century, compared with the 1990s when approximately half of all English undergraduate students were over 25 years of age.

Who teaches in higher education?

If we move to a brief consideration of the people who attend university from the teaching side, the academic workforce in the UK increased 20 per cent over the 10 year period, 1995–2005, as student numbers increased. The total number of full-time equivalent academic staff has grown over the period by nearly 17 000 to

97 000. Within this decade to 2005, the proportion of women in academic posts also rose by 9 per cent to 36 per cent, just over a third of all academics; yet it remains the case that, while most students taking English are women, most academics teaching English are men. It is interesting also to observe that the proportion of women professors in HE has doubled over this time span – although from a low starting point – from 9 per cent of the total to 19 per cent. The indications are that this upward trend will continue (although there is a long lead time as few academics are appointed to professorial posts before their 40s).

This improvement in career progression for women could be the result of rising proportions of women attending and studying at universities and colleges in recent decades. Other underrepresented groups are also increasing in number and HEIs are now recruiting in a global marketplace, which is reflected in the increasingly multinational academic workforce. Consequently, there is also a rising trend in the proportion of academic staff from black and minority ethnic backgrounds, rising by 2 percentage points to 8 per cent of the total – mostly attributable to an increase in the numbers of Asian staff, especially Indian and Chinese.

Finally, universities and HE colleges employ not just academics, and in total there were 284 000 people employed in 130 HEIs in England in 2004–5. More than 1 per cent of the total workforce in the UK works in HE if we include professional and support staff as well as academic employees.

What are the key skills for English studies?

In 2002, the English Subject Centre asked English departments to comment on the student profile at their institutions (www.english.heacademy.ac.uk/) and some views expressed in responses were common across the sector: for example, that weaknesses of written expression and organization are on the rise and that there is an increasing decline in the standard of literacy, even among those with high A-level grades. This is an important factor in the transition many students will need to make successfully from pre-university study to HE, where the amount of reading and the speed with which lecturers expect them to study texts may come as a surprise. In an age when there are so many calls on people's time, there is thus some concern among teaching staff about the depth and extent of students' knowledge and their capacity for independent learning. This is partly to say lecturers perceive that there is a greater reliance on approaches and readings provided by teaching staff themselves, with fewer students exhibiting an inclination towards independent research. It has been suggested that this is a result of the modern and somewhat instrumentalist emphasis on assessment in education, which encourages students to be more conservative in their approach to assignments because of a fear of failure if they rely too much on imagination and initiative, even though these are often the characteristics of original thought that markers value.

In essence, if you are preparing for university-level English, you are best advised to concentrate on the breadth of your reading, in terms of knowledge and understanding, and the quality of your writing, in terms of skills. These two elements, combined with a lively, genuine interest and an enquiring, reflective mind, are the surest foundations for success. English students are generally highly praised in terms of their abilities and well placed for most subsequent careers because of the range of general knowledge and analytical skills inculcated by English studies.

How will you be taught?

Teaching takes place over three levels (or four in Scotland), which are most commonly taken full-time over the same number of years. Hence you will find people referring to level 1, 2 and 3. Level 1 is usually introductory and the threshold achievement you need to attain, in terms of progressing to level 2, is a pass, although most students will aim to do considerably better. Levels 2 and 3 are the 'honours' years where your final degree classification will be established through the marks you receive for the assessed work you undertake – the balance between levels 2 and 3 in determining your result varies greatly between universities. Your honours degree will be denoted by a class: first, upper or lower second, or third. In recent years, about 10 per cent of students achieve the distinction of a first, and nearly all the others receive a second, with only a minority now leaving higher education with a third-class degree. The 'with honours' (latin: *cum laude*) component most commonly rests on taking the final year dissertation or project module, which is offered by the majority of departments and is often deemed the most important piece of work in terms of academic endeavour and in terms of achieving success. Some students decide not to take this module and may thus elect to receive a degree without honours.

The most common diet of teaching is a balance of lectures and group discussion classes (usually seminars of varied group sizes). Although a large number will have roughly half and half, many institutions will have more classes than lectures; only a few will have more lectures. The full range of teaching methods includes: consultations in tutors' weekly 'office hours'; tutorials for the dissertation project (one to one discussions with the tutor); seminars with between ten and 30 students; group presentations, usually within a seminar; practical sessions, especially in creative writing; essay tutorials with up to five students; sessions in IT classrooms (the use of virtual learning environments and e-learning are increasingly common); student-led classes; distance-learning or mobile-learning (m-learning) packages; and on-line discussion groups.

As to the length of time spent each week in classes, or those periods where undergraduates receive formal tuition from staff, the average is between six and ten hours a week but might be as high as 15. With regard to private study, average hours per week are usually between 20 and 30 hours. In most (but not all) institutions, the amount of assessment by formal examination on a programme ranges from 21 per cent to 50 per cent, with the rest given over to continuous assessment.

Most universities and/or departments provide an extensive pastoral network for students, the aim of which is to help enhance the 'student experience', which is a current buzz-phrase in HE. Specialist advice is available in many areas as well as academic: accommodation; child care; careers; counselling; finance; medical matters; support for disabled students. There are other bodies to help too, from the chaplaincy to the students' union. You may also have the opportunity to study in other countries on Socrates/Erasmus or Brethren Colleges Abroad programmes.

How will English help you in later life?

Remember that English is multi-vocational rather than non-vocational and many of the skills that are necessary to graduate in

English are highly prized in every job or profession, with students able to perform a range of important tasks: to write well in a variety of formats; to organize workloads and work to tight deadlines; to convey meaning precisely; to summarize, argue and debate within contexts; to interpret, assess and evaluate sources; to develop opinions, propose ideas and theories; to think logically and laterally; to absorb and retain large amounts of information; to persuade others of a point of view; to think and act creatively. This is an impressive skills set and it is helpful to reflect on the abilities you are developing in this way; your institution will probably also have in place a personal development plan (PDP) programme which will encourage you to build up a portfolio of your achievements under a variety of headings.

Traditionally, teaching has been an important career area for English graduates who wish to use their subject. To teach in state schools in the UK you need to complete a one-year Postgraduate Certificate in Education (PGCE) for which early application in your final year is needed. Teaching English as a foreign language (TEFL) may require the completion of a short course, although many graduates teach abroad with no formal teaching qualification. The media, an area which interests many English graduates, are now offering more opportunities than in previous years but usually graduates need to gain relevant work experience (voluntary or paid) or follow a one-year vocational course to succeed in this competitive area. This may explain why more English graduates initially enter management or administrative roles than journalism or writing.

It is still true that many English graduates regard the subject matter of their degree as essentially irrelevant when making their career choice and happily investigate the full range of occupations. English graduates are very adaptable, often pursuing less obvious routes to their chosen destinations or moving from one employment sector to another. Many begin their careers in administrative roles, others enter financial careers, work in management in the private sector, train to become teachers, social workers or lawyers, or work in local government and the Civil Service. Good communication skills, which are often developed by studying English, are highly valued by employers. If you are thinking about future careers, the best place to start considering your options as a graduate is the prospects website at: www.prospects.ac.uk

It is also possible to study at postgraduate level in subjects both directly related and unrelated to your first degree. It is important that you begin investigating opportunities for postgraduate study early and in most instances application should be made directly to the institution concerned. There is no guarantee of funding for postgraduate study and it is often easier to obtain a place than it is to secure finance. This is particularly true for arts graduates. The Arts and Humanities Research Council is the funding body concerned with postgraduate awards in English. Competition for awards is fierce, so it is worth exploring other potential sources of funding.

What is on the curriculum?

English is a diverse and constantly changing subject in which critical self-awareness is perhaps the most important element. It covers study of the English language and of the literatures of not only Great Britain and Ireland, but also of other countries from the Anglophone world. 'English studies' can also incorporate in its curriculum comparative literature and literature in translation, plus non-literary texts, as well as the study and practice of drama, creative writing and film.

Over 90 per cent of HEIs offer Single Honours English, but most also offer English with another subject as Combined or Joint Honours. The largest changes in the last ten years have been that more language teaching is in the curriculum and there has been an enormous growth in creative writing courses, which has had a substantial effect on the shape of English studies nationwide. The majority of courses have at least some compulsory elements, of which the most common are in these areas: introductions to the study of English and/or literature at degree level; critical/literary theory; literary history; literary genres; and critical practice.

The number of optional courses is generally higher than the number of compulsory courses. 'Late twentieth century and contemporary' and 'modernist' are the most widely available options, with 'renaissance' coming third. 'Critical/literary theory' is the most widely taught compulsory course, with 'general linguistics' in second place. In terms of the way in which the syllabus foundations are shaped, the following indicate the curriculum choices made by departments, from most influential to least: coverage of literary periods; reading/interpretive skills; specialist interests of staff; giving student choice; coverage of literary history; genre study; theoretical issues; language/linguistic study; theme-based courses; cultural history; individual authors; and cultural politics. The most popular courses are contemporary literature, creative writing, film, modernism, Shakespeare and women's writing. Amongst 'global' English, Irish literature is the most widely taught.[2]

From this, you will get a flavour of the kinds of areas and specialisms you might encounter. To make sure that you will be studying aspects of English that you feel might appeal to you, it is worth looking at the curriculum of any department to which you are thinking of applying. Some students only find out after they have enrolled that the diet of teaching and learning on offer on their first-year syllabus is not to their taste, by which time it is far less easy to change to another choice of course.

What are the characteristics of English studies?

In the UK, a 'subject benchmark statement' for the honours degree was produced for English in 2000 by academics from across the country for the Quality Assurance Agency (QAA – see www.qaa.ac.uk/academicinfrastructure/benchmark/statements/English07.asp). Subject benchmark statements, which have now been developed for most disciplines, provide a means for the academic community to describe the nature and characteristics of programmes in a specific subject and the standards of degree awards, plus the attributes and capabilities graduates should possess.

Revised in 2007, the English statement characterizes the subject as, above all, a versatile academic discipline focused on 'the production, reception and interpretation of written texts' and 'the nature, history and potential of the English language'. The study of English literature and language should aim towards encouraging an openness of mind, conceptual sophistication, and a vibrant dialogue with past and present cultures and values, and as a student you 'are expected to be aware of the production and determination of meaning by historical, social, political, stylistic, ethnic, gender, geographical and other contexts'.

The document covers the key subject-specific, generic and transferable skills an English graduate should attain, and you may wish to view these on-line, but I should like to say a little more about levels of attainment and standards. Most fundamentally, an averagely successful English student will be able to demonstrate an extensive knowledge of the subject expressed in an appropriate critical vocabulary and through an effective command of written English. With respect to understanding, literature, graduates should also be able to make connections between a substantial range of authors, texts and genres from different historical periods or cultures, while language graduates should be able to explain coherently and cogently a range of approaches to the study of English language. In terms of skills, English students will generally be able to interpret different ideas, critical approaches and values. However, English also aims to develop both powers of textual analysis and of fluent critical argument.

A report by the Council for Industry for Higher Education, titled 'Employability: employer perceptions of subject benchmark statements', found with regard to English that '70%+ responding employers recognise that critical thinking, communication skills, learning and self development and creativity are competences that are being developed'. Moreover, some of the employers surveyed also thought that studying English developed a number of other qualities and attributes that were not in the benchmark statement: persuasiveness, drive, judgement, conceptual thinking and confidence (see www.cihe-uk.com/docs/PUBS/forbes.pdf).

It can be concluded from this that the skills English students display are as varied as the discipline, but that key skills of writing, analysis, communication, and critical and creative thinking are at the core of the subject. These are far from non-vocational skills, of course, and will stand you in good stead in the employment market.

2 English studies

The experience of English in higher education strikes new students in different ways depending on the educational background they come from and the HE institution they attend. However, there are some important areas that surface time and again for those adjusting to the different demands of study at this level. In this chapter we will look at four aspects of English at university level: the first is the range of reading and study; the second is the texts you are most likely to encounter; the third is the broad area of theory, of historical contexts, and of critical approaches to English studies; and the fourth is the fraught question of language and meaning.

Breadth and depth

For students who come direct from further education, often the most striking difference at university level is the requirement to read more material in a shorter space of time. Although there are opportunities for more detailed study at various points on a number of courses, students' reading schedules will now seem much more heavily loaded, and you will need to develop the skills to deal with this as soon as possible. You may also find you are asked to read more criticism, both as a means to promote debate and to introduce different schools of theoretical and critical thought. Tutors will be keen to promote independent study and encourage your reflective thinking both within the discipline of English and, in many cases, across the disciplines. Their concern will therefore be to provide you with the intellectual framework and the reading skills required for proficient 'critical practice'.

The main educational aims of English programmes are to provide opportunities for students to develop a sound knowledge of forms and conventions alongside the ability to read, debate, and write knowledgeably about texts with skill and flair. To do this you must acquire a critical vocabulary adequate to the understanding and analysis of complex forms of language while establishing a general ability to think independently and reflectively upon your learning. Which is to say, you need to read as widely as possible and reflect on the connections between different books, ideas, authors and approaches to texts.

All universities and colleges will have either a library or, increasingly now, a learning resources centre, which is geared as much towards the use of information and communications technology as paper-based texts, and will have spaces for small-group work as well as for solitary reading. Almost all HEIs will provide optional or compulsory library instruction at levels 1 and/or 2. Essay writing skills at level 1 are also compulsory for the majority of institutions, usually provided by the department, with optional instruction available at later levels. It is only slightly less common these days for departments to provide some training in oral communication or presentation skills. You will also find great emphasis placed on the academic presentation of work, including such aspects as referencing and bibliographic conventions. Some instruction in this important scholarly area is compulsory at almost all institutions, while computer and internet training is nearly always available too, and some HEIs will provide software packages for teaching and learning aspects of English language.[1]

To understand how you learn, and how you learn best, is the hardest educational task for all students. It is also not something that most people think about. There are several different learning styles and it is also true that we all learn holistically, in many life contexts, not just when we think we are studying. For example, your dominant learning style might be auditory, visual or kinaesthetic and tactile (learning by doing): there are many tools on-line for you to work out which you are; for example the support4learning.co.uk website has useful materials, including a link to a simple chart to help you assess your own learning style at www.chaminade.org/inspire/learnstl.htm

Texts studied

Each English course is distinctive and reflects the interests and expertise of staff in the department. It is also true, however, that, as the English Benchmarking statement states, 'the overall structure, the relationship between the individual elements, and objectives of the course as a whole, should be coherent and explicit'. The courses and modules offered in English studies often largely allow you to compile your own diet of study according to your needs and interests. For instance, it may be possible for you to construct a programme based broadly on a conventional mainstream of English literature, or on period studies largely arranged in chronological sequence. The flexibility and range of options on courses is worth checking in advance, just as it is also important to ask yourself early on how you would prefer to structure your course around particular aspects or approaches to English language, or studies of writings that have not been commonly included on traditional English literature courses. Most courses will offer modules in American literature, literatures in English and in a variety of writings by women; but all courses will differ and have their own specialisms; for example, English teaching teams may have a strong commitment to either the canon of 'great works' or the study of 'minority'/'marginalized' writings. At my own institution, for example, we firmly believe that the study of under-represented writings will enhance and enrich your understanding of both literature and literary studies, as well as assisting your understanding of the way that a literary canon is established and perpetuated. This is one of the much-debated sides to English study in literature and you will want to decide for yourself which is more important to you: an opportunity to study literary 'classics', or texts by diverse authors that may be new to you.

'Theory' and the importance of history

In the 1980s and especially the 1990s, literary theory was a dominant aspect of critical study. After the so-called 'theory wars' of the 1990s, in the 2000s theory has found an integrated place within the spectrum of literary analysis. It is less frequent for someone strongly to identify themselves in terms of theoretical positions such as feminism, Marxism or post-structuralism, but an awareness of these schools of thought features in almost all published literary criticism and an understanding of 'theory' within the spectrum of critical approaches is probably only second in importance to an understanding of literary history and context. Indeed, one of the most attractive features of an English degree is the opportunity it offers you to reflect on your own experiences and views in critical ways, as one student explained in an interview with the English Subject Centre: 'The course is not just about [reading "classic" literature], it also covers critical theory and gives you more confidence in what you are thinking, [making you] more open to other things.'[2]

The first point to make about theory is that it argues that we always do have a critical approach to the study of literature even though we do not necessarily always think that we do. 'Traditional' literary criticism takes itself to be apolitical, disinterested, neutral and even perhaps 'natural'. Yet, any approach to literature, if it is to be replicated, must have a set of assumptions if not principles, and this is the place we should start.

The most common 'traditional' approach to literary study can be outlined by the following six points:

1   Meaning lies with the author. The novel or poem has varied meanings to different readers but there is only one true meaning – that which the author intended. It is the author's imagination and moral feeling that we are appreciating in reading literature. George Eliot said that great art 'enlarges our sympathies', and, in line with this, traditional criticism thinks good literature educates our sensibilities.

2   Popular literature is that which is ephemeral and merely contemporary, whereas good literature conveys and embodies timeless qualities and values: it is that which communicates universally and transcends its time of writing. We ought to note here also that literature is supposed to be well-written, but good writing alone does not always constitute literature – otherwise a diversity of texts such as history books, philosophical essays and religious sermons would more often be called literature – as indeed might menus, advertisements and magazines. It is worth thinking here what actually does constitute literature – for example, are the works of Charles

Darwin and Sigmund Freud literature? Is the Bible, the Koran or Greek mythology? Can biographies be literature? If so, which and why?

3   The way to read literature is through habits of what are called close reading and practical criticism. This usually means, on the one hand paying attention to the formal qualities of the text (its use of metaphors, rhymes, images and repetitions) and on the other hand employing our emotion, aesthetic response and sense of moral values to respond to it. Literary study requires sensitivity, understanding and feeling rather than an attention to its extra-textual contexts. Literature is moral but not political, humane but not didactic.

4   The most important aspects to attend to in studying a novel are literary language, plot and character. In reading a novel we ask such questions as are the characters well-rounded and believable? Do they act as real people do? Is any of the plot superfluous? Is the ending well prepared for, and does the beginning make sense of what comes afterwards? Incidentally, these are not modern questions but concerns that go back to the Greek philosophers. Plato and Aristotle disagreed about whether plot or character was more important to imaginative writing, and Henry James and H.G. Wells had the same argument.

5   A good poem or piece of prose is one with a unified whole meaning in which all the parts fit together – nothing is unnecessary and everything adds to the sense of the poem or the plot of the novel.

6   Last, the question such criticism asks is: *what* does the literary work mean?

An alternative approach to the one above begins with the premise that all (economic, social, cultural and even personal) action is linked to the operations of power and is therefore political. Literature, in terms of its production, consumption and interpretation, is consequently also political.

Perhaps the first thing to say about political theory is that it does not view literature as timeless and universal. Instead, it maintains that novels and poems are rooted in history, and texts will reveal various 'ideologies' that lie behind them. So what is 'ideology'? In a traditional sense it is of course a political persuasion, a consciously held set of beliefs about something; but this only gives a narrow definition of 'ideology' and is the definition favoured by those who think they do not have an ideology. Critical theory argues by contrast that everyone has an 'ideological perspective', which is in Terry Eagleton's words 'the largely concealed structure of values which informs and underlies our factual statements'.[3] So, ideology is not just the politics we hold, the prejudices we show, and the opinions that we put forward, it is our entire (imaginary) relationship with the real conditions of our existence, and so is most clearly shown not in what we preach but what we practise: for example, the ideology of 'freedom' promotes the belief in the liberty of everyone, but in capitalist society there is actually a complex mesh of power relationships restricting people's lives at all points, most clearly in relation to access to such things as money or work. Similarly, the ideology that maintains 'people are basically the same' serves to deny or obscure the enormous differences in the social and economic conditions that distinguish people's lives. So, as an illustration, traditional approaches to literature ask us to consider the universal facts of birth, death and suffering – to create empathy with the characters' lives through a perception of shared experience. However, the conditions under which women give birth, and the circumstances under which people suffer, are extremely varied and an appreciation of these differences will affect our perceptions and emotions. We also have to pay attention to different ways of reading fiction because of our divergent perspectives. For example, in *Jane Eyre* Charlotte Brontë illustrates the ways in which Jane is necessarily restricted by the male-dominated society around her because she has no financial independence – only inheritance can change this for her. From a feminist perspective this highlights the oppression suffered in Victorian society by women – especially those without money or advanced social status (even in marriage all a wife's assets legally became her husband's). On the other hand, from a different political perspective, what the novel omits to discuss at any length is the source of that fortune – Jane inherits the wealth that her uncle has acquired from his vineyards in Madeira. The inheritance marks Jane's liberation in English patriarchal society, but her emancipation rests on the suffering and exploitation of slave workers elsewhere.

Ideology, far from being conscious, is most effective in its influence on us when we are unaware of its operation. Its effect is to naturalize or normalize existing relations – we generally are encouraged to think of the social relations we participate in as in some way unchangeable or usual or right. Perhaps one trivial example from Jane Austen's novel *Emma* can illustrate what I mean. At the start of Chapter 49 there is the following description: 'The weather continued much the same all the following morning; and the same loneliness, and the same melancholy, seemed to reign at Hartfield . . .'. Crudely speaking, if the weather complements the mood of the characters in novels, this conceit is generally praised – thought of as a literary technique that blends the description of the weather with the emotions of the characters to show nature and humanity in accord. What it also does, however, is suggest that human society and conditions are a part of the natural world: are to be expected and tolerated because that is the way of things. We may believe that we are less happy when there is bad weather, but this is precisely how ideology operates upon us to normalize our cultural behaviour. It is not such a long step from this perspective to one that attributes people's character to the climate and reduces their personalities to stereotypical traits such as a Mediterranean temperament or a reserved northern manner.

One immediate observation we can make is that literature works to create an ideological perspective in the reader and this is reinforced by traditional literary criticism. We are asked, as readers, to identify with the characters, to reflect their values, accept their beliefs. If, as in *Emma*, the characters are resentful and distrustful of change, then this fosters a degree of conservatism in the reader also. A novel that tells us that money, power and class are not as important as family, romantic love and individual happiness, whether we agree with it or not, is transmitting an ideology: it encourages readers to accept their position in the social order and direct their energies towards personal goals rather than political ones. As will now be apparent, the term 'political' here does not refer just to party politics and views on such events as the Iraq War, but every aspect of our lives – anywhere that a relationship of influence is in operation from the effects of racial attacks and sexual harassment to the views we express about the novels we read.

If we are aware of and conscious to the workings of ideology in a text, then our approach to literature may be affected in three ways:

1   First, we can look at the text to assess the ideology of the author and his or her time.

2   Second, we can consider the production of literature more widely. For example, critics argue that the novel form itself reveals a particular kind of ideology, that of the middle classes. Its emphasis on the life-like representation of the existence of 'rounded individuals' is the very substance of bourgeois ideology from a Marxist viewpoint: it reinforces the values of individualism, free enterprise and a class structure in which the interdependence of different classes is downplayed. This is not just a question of politics but one of history. The novel, as an art form, arises in the eighteenth century at the same time as industrial capitalism, which is to say in a changing society that no longer sees itself as primarily communal and collective, but as containing free, competitive, independent and private individuals. The activity of novel-reading, which is solitary, unlike drama, singing and the recital of poetry, reinforces individualism in society.

3   Last, we can consider our own ideology – when reading through a novel, what do we attend to in thinking about or analysing the text, and how do we write about it – what do we discuss as important, and why?

Political theory offers many different answers to this last question, but we can look at three approaches here that are particularly prominent, and which focus respectively on gender, class and colonialism.

Gender

Austen's novel *Emma* suggests that marriage is an object in life and an ending in fiction. The novel insinuates that the main preoccupation of a young woman's thoughts should be marriage. This effect is primarily achieved through 'closure', a term used to describe the way of finishing a novel with a sense of ends tied up. 'Closure' is ideologically important because it suggests that the rest of the novel has been leading inevitably up to this point: that whatever happens at the end is in some sense 'correct'. The more formally structured a novel is, the stronger this ideological effect will be. In Austen's novels, the main plots always end happily and this is united to an idea about moral worth and growth. The connection between morality and happiness suggests that if we are good, if we conform to society's dictates, we will achieve happiness. The emphasis in *Emma* on marriage also suggests that a woman's life is defined by her passage from one man, her father, to another, her husband. Her father, Mr Woodhouse, and eventual husband, Mr Knightley, clearly occupy positions of dominance, even though Emma believes she can be mistress of their houses, and the novel is explicit in its belief in the importance of family life, the obligation to respect one's parents, and the necessity of chastity.

Feminist approaches to literature predominantly take one of three forms:

1   The recuperation of marginalized women's writing (e.g. by such publishers as Virago and The Women's Press).
2   The analysis of gender relations and representations in literature.
3   A consideration of whether writing has itself become a practice defined as masculine. Just as the generic term 'man' has in the past supposedly included women, but really made women invisible, perhaps also the structure and tone of writing has been shaped by men, because it has been dominated by them. Some women authors have therefore written exclusively about women's experience and also attempted to give birth to a different kind of prose – one that is less controlled, formal and structured, more fluid, personal and creative.

Class

In *Emma* class barriers or wealth do not *appear* insuperable impediments to individuals from poor classes and this allows us to equalize in the imagination what is unequal in society. The marriages at the end of the novel are made to appear 'right' or 'natural', but we should also observe that they reinforce the existing class structures. Harriet cannot marry Knightley; the thought deeply offends Emma, and although Austen portrays Emma as a snob, the character was also Austen's favourite heroine; do the marriages at the end of the novel suggest that Austen, like her society, is equally disinclined to countenance marriage across classes? The novel implies characters will get the marriage partners they deserve, and Austen's matches

are based less on romance than on social and economic considerations, tied to moral worth. Fanny Price and Edmund Bertram
end up together at the close of *Mansfield Park* because on the
one hand Fanny, although a poor relation, has the same breeding,
and on the other because they have both in some sense earned one
another. The novel charts their moral development and education
until Austen considers they are right for each other. Similarly,
Emma has to mature sufficiently to both appreciate and win her
'Knight'.

Another curious fact of note with *Emma* is the novel's dedication
to the Prince Regent, who was a great admirer of Austen's novels.
On the one hand, we know that Austen disliked him and therefore
it is not a personal dedication but a formal one; on the other hand,
the fact that so hated a member of the Royal Family could identify
with and praise her novels, and be in turn honoured by one of them,
reinforces a reading that wants to argue there is a deeply conservative ideology at work in Austen's fiction (e.g. contrast this with
Shelley's excoriating poem on the monarchy 'England in 1819',
just three years later).

Austen's novels tease away at the morals and manners of the
middle-class country gentry, and are thus mostly unconcerned
with the aristocracy or the peasantry. The scene in which Harriet
encounters the gypsies in *Emma* is interesting because the threat
they pose to her is similar to the threat they pose to the novel as a
whole. The gypsies are kept at the margins of the plot (almost
ignored, as are servants) and the possibility of their disrupting the
social order is similarly repressed – only a year before Waterloo and
two decades on from the French Revolution. These incidents on
the world stage are of course for the most part also unmentioned in
Austen's novels (the military are less fighters than potential hus-
bands), and their omission is significant because it could be argued
to represent an attempt to deny or avoid history. The conservative
message about the French Revolution of Austen's novels is perhaps
that 'it can't happen here', yet the time in which she was writing
was a period of great unrest in Britain and abroad. Probably the
only allusion to this we have in *Emma* is at the start of Chapter 20,
when we learn that Jane Fairfax's father was an infantry soldier who
'died in action abroad'.

If we compare this attitude with similarly lauded canonical

French or Russian novels, the lack of historical engagement in Austen's fiction is striking – a point which, given that these contemporaries are nearly all men, might take us back to the necessity for a feminist approach to inform our reading of the novel.

The point here is that what is pushed to a novel's margins or left out altogether is just as important, ideologically, as what is put in. Austen discusses the morals of a class but she does this by turning within, not looking without. In consequence, by examining one class it might be argued she is actually examining no classes. The observation to be made here is one about definition, which is extremely important to literary theory. Theory argues that something is known through not identity but difference. We can only know what *white* is by considering it in relation to *black*, what *man* is by considering its relation to *woman*, what the *middle classes* are by reference to *other classes*. And, consequently, by discussing only the middle class, Austen will never sufficiently discuss them: what the middle class is can only be defined by considering the relationships between the classes.

Colonialism

The above discussion takes us to a third political aspect that we ought to attend to, but which at first sight seems less than important to novels such as Austen's. Most succinctly put: we only know what England is or what Europe is by considering each of them in relation to the rest of the world. Austen's *Mansfield Park*, and E.M. Forster's *Howards End* (1910), as another example, are novels about English life and gentility that belong to a long tradition where the eponymous houses are representative of wider society. The debate over the English country-house novel is one that concerns itself with the 'Condition of England', as it came to be known in the 1840s – with the morals, manners, characters and values of English society. However, both the societies and the families discussed in these novels are economically dependent on the development of the British Empire and on overseas 'trade' – trade here largely being a euphemism for colonial exploitation. These aspects are not foregrounded in the novel, and they are not commonly discussed by critics, but this is itself an ideologically significant omission. British colonialism is considered unimportant because it is marginal in the novel's textual discussion. Sir Thomas Bertram in *Mansfield Park* is the source and fount of authority; he is both the law and the moral order in the house. When he is abroad, regulated discipline and puritan soberliness are gently challenged by the frivolity, romance and profligacy of the younger generation, under the spell of the Crawfords. The climax of this is of course to be the play, the ethical status of which troubles Fanny Price so much. Fortunately for Fanny, the book's moral conscience, Sir Thomas returns in time to restore order and propriety.

Yet, where has Sir Thomas been? The answer is to his plantations in Antigua where he has been similarly ruling and controlling the local community. And in fact the regulated harmony of *Mansfield Park* is dependent on Sir Thomas also holding sway on his plantation in Antigua – where, as it so happens, the early nineteenth century was a time of serious economic problems, slave revolts and colonial competition with France. Antigua economically sustains Mansfield Park and both places are controlled by and for wealth – in Antigua its production, in *Mansfield Park* its consumption. Both communities are also to do with rule – with the maintenance of the *status quo*, with the right to rule, and with the appropriate sense of proper behaviour that accompanies a hierarchical social order. But there is a striking discrepancy, even an incompatibility, between the refined moral sense that Austen delineates in the Bertram household and the basic conditions of slavery imposed in the West Indies. The point here is not that Austen ought to criticize her society but that the society we witness in *Mansfield Park* is a slave-owning one, whose moral as well as material well-being is founded – contentedly – on the cruelty and inhumanity of the sugar trade of the period and on enforced slave labourers transported from Africa to a Caribbean island. A century later, African 'trade' supports *Howards End* too.

Language and textual theory

I conjectured earlier on the question of what texts we might consider to be 'literature'? If you spend any time thinking about this question you will soon find it is almost impossible to answer satisfactorily. Political theory will say that 'literature' is an ideological construct – like everything else in society, the concept of literature is determined by 'power' and vested interests (including institutions like universities).

Another response, however, would query the concept behind the word 'literature'. The concept itself relies on the notion of a 'canon' and the kind of reading practice I outlined earlier – it seems to require that there are *good* books and *bad* books. It also implies three ideological positions: that the things to attend to in a novel are not history and culture but character and plot; that literature enriches our cultural lives more than other writing; and that the important guarantor of meaning is the intention of the author who produced the work of literature. However, if we interrogate these ideas then we will, at the same time, be questioning the category of 'literature' altogether. If we move to studying not what the text says but how it says it and if we analyse metaphors not for their imaginativeness but for what they imply, then surely the things that we study when we do 'English' are present in all texts.

Undoubtedly, what is present in all literature is writing. So, to many critics, the most important aspect to analyse is actually the movement and play of 'language', or what is called 'textuality'. When studying a novel, for example, we need not ask what characters or authors mean, but we do need to ask what words mean and, as importantly, how do they mean? The context becomes the most important thing here: what language *means* is not fixed by the author but is produced by the particular reader from the written text within a historical context. Earlier I said that we can only know what something is by considering it in relation to what it is defined against, by what it is not. This is actually where literary theory begins. It starts of course with language, but we need to know what language is. Traditionally linguists chiefly studied language diachronically, which means across time. They studied the development of a language and how its usages changed in speech communities and from generation to generation. At the start of the twentieth century, however, linguists began to consider language synchronically – in one time period – and ask how people used language at any one time. Two important points were deduced.

First comes the point that linguistic referentiality is not best represented by the relation between a 'word' and a 'thing', but between a 'signifier' (or symbol) and a 'signified' (or concept). There is thus a SYMBOL and a CONCEPT but no connection in language between the SYMBOL and the world, or what we call 'reality'. So, a signifier's meaning is dependent on context:

e.g. 'Cat' means a four-legged domestic furry animal, but it also denotes:
>   the general name for a genus of animals including lions and tigers
>   a rope-whip on a ship
>   a woman
>   a tripod
>   etc.

If we put 'cat' in other contexts, like the expressions 'cat got your tongue' or 'hell-cat' or 'raining cats and dogs' it has very different meanings. Language uses these different meanings constantly; and this is particularly foregrounded by literary study. So, to choose a much-discussed phrase, consider the opening to Keats's 'Ode on a Grecian Urn': '*Thou still unravish'd bride of quietness.*' In this phrase, the word 'still' means 'not moving', because the Grecian urn is motionless, as is the scene that is depicted on it, but it also means 'not yet'. The urn remains metaphorically unravished – suggesting on one level simply that it is unbroken. As the poem develops we find new meanings and contexts (marriage, silence, vows, sex) for the other words too because, evidently, the urn is not in fact a 'bride' and is certainly not married to quietness in any conventional sense, and so on. This quality of plural meanings has been thought to be a property of literary language, but it certainly is not exclusively so by any means. It is a property of all language. The word 'still' has different meanings no matter who uses it and any words can be shifted into new contexts that provide new meanings. Consequently, the way we understand or interpret 'literature' and all writing reveals our preoccupations and cultural concerns as readers, not what the text means in any definitive sense. 'Literary' language is more a property of the process of reading texts than a property of a separate category of writing, although we might argue that some texts provoke more, and more interesting, readings than others.

Second comes the point that language is *arbitrary* and works through *difference* not equivalence. For example, with a set of traffic lights, which is a simple language or code, red means 'stop' and green means 'go' – to those who know the code. But there is no necessary reason for this arrangement. We could reverse the colours;

or blue could be used to mean 'stop' and orange to mean 'go'. The same applies to language – there is no reason why 'cat' should mean a four-legged animal – any word (or signifier) will do. That is, any symbol will suffice as long as it is distinguishable from every other symbol. The same is true with traffic lights: it does not matter which colours are used just so long as they are distinguishable and known. Consequently, we may say that language means what it does through 'difference'. 'Cat' means what it does because it is distinguishable from 'dog' and 'cap' and 'bat', not because it bears any relation to a four-legged animal.

This is actually one of the most radical developments in thinking in the last century. Primarily it is important because it asserts the social nature of language. I said that *we* could agree to reverse the traffic lights signs for stop and go; but who is 'we'? Individuals or groups can do it themselves easily but unless it is *socially* and *collectively* agreed then we are going to have a lot of accidents! On the one hand, language is 'immutable', 'unchangeable' – the relation between red and 'stop' in wider society is fixed as far as we are concerned as individuals. However, language is also 'mutable' or 'changeable' because words do change their meanings over time. But this is only within a collective system. The conclusion to this may be that we should pay as much attention to the use of language in society as to the use of language by an author. Also, the fact that language is a system that gives rise to meaning through differences is particularly important if we extend the idea to other realms of meaning. So, for example, we can again ask 'what is literature?' We know that one answer is to cite great literary works that communicate timeless human values. Another response, however, is to say that by 'literature' what is meant is that which is not 'minor' or 'popular' or 'genre' writing, and so on. Similarly, a *marital* status of 'married' is most meaningful because it signifies 'not single', 'not divorced', 'not widowed': like 'red' at a traffic-lights party, the wedding ring signifies 'not available'. And of course the status of 'married' would have no meaning without the other signifiers, which is to say that the other conceptual categories are referred to or implied by the word 'married'. Language therefore functions in the fashion of an 'alibi', which is primarily significant for its differentiation from another possibility. An alibi is not important because it says where you were at a certain time, but because it says that you were *not* present at the scene of a crime. So, with language we can attend to the words that are not used, and the inferences we can make, when a government spokesperson describes the long-term unemployed as 'economically inactive', or a butcher is only referred to as a 'purveyor of meat'.

Last, another implication of a theory that says language only *means* through differences between signifiers/words, is that when we speak, when we write and when we read literature, all we have is language. If I give you a new word – let us say 'interpellation' – I have almost no way of telling you what that word means without using other words, which are themselves defined by other words (I can of course use another sign-system, such as charades, but I cannot break free from signifiers).

As an exercise, ask yourself what 'horse' means; decide on your answer (or use the definition in the dictionary) and then consider the following five comments:

1   Presumably you have thought of other words, or perhaps pictures; but you have not attempted to round up all the 'real' (and imaginary) horses that there are.
2   So the word 'horse' does not mean anything on its own – it 'means' all these other symbols/words/signifiers in your definition. And if we pick any of the defining words, they again only have a meaning elsewhere, in further words.
3   'Horse' does not make meaning through its relation to the world, but through its relation to words or other signifiers.
4   The same is true of 'black', 'love', 'England', etc.
5   Meaning is never present to itself – it is always *in other words*.

Similarly, when we think about anything, all we have is language. All we have are words that we did not invent and which mostly existed before we did. They are words we have been given and which we then speak. The result of this is that we are located in language. We are in the 'prison-house' of language as one critic puts it; which means that we also have to change our view of what language does as well as what it is. Traditional criticism argues that we use words to reflect or at least represent reality. We have an experience or a thought and then we express ourselves through language. 'Theory' argues, however, that this is the wrong way around. Language comes first – it exists before we do and once we have been *given* language and taught the way to play with it, it becomes transparent and natural to us. Language therefore exists before any of our experiences do and consequently we do not express ourselves through language – language is expressed through us. It is language that for human purposes constructs what we call 'reality' – it does not reflect it.

This is where much theory actually begins, but it is such a radical idea that I thought it would be a better place to end: there will be plenty of opportunity when studying English to debate this approach to language and literature.

3 Culture and society[1]

English does not exist in a vacuum, and you might want to consider English literature, creative writing and English language as a family of subjects within the one area of study. You might also want to consider taking more than one of them as a joint or combined degree, but there are other subjects that students frequently choose to combine with one of them. The most common of these are fellow humanities and social science subjects such as politics, history, psychology, religious studies and philosophy, or cultural studies courses, including American and women's studies, or arts and media courses.

When writing the Subject Benchmark Statement for English discussed in the previous chapter, its authors stated clearly that in framing the statement they had 'been sensitive to the fact that English has strong affiliations with several complementary disciplines, including Linguistics, Drama, Communication Studies and Philosophy, and that there are cases where disciplinary boundaries overlap'. English studies ought to be an interdisciplinary subject and arguably it is implicitly one even when course descriptions do not make this explicit. So, for example, when asked if their courses provide the opportunity for interdisciplinary work 79 per cent of departments replied affirmatively.[2]

In fact, it could be argued that English is an area of study in which almost all the other disciplines can legitimately be discussed. History is crucial to a full understanding of language, for example. Philosophy is similarly the basis of some literary works, and many others are largely incomprehensible without an understanding of key religious texts. Psychology shares a discourse with literature, not least through the emphasis on analysis and the study of mental processes, while sociology and cultural studies clearly overlap with the socio-cultural aspects to studying both literature and language.

In terms of interdisciplinarity within joint honours or within English single honours, you are most likely to encounter a syllabus that overlaps with history or media studies (especially film). However, according to surveys of departments, you may find that an English degree contains an interdisciplinary element related to any of these subjects: philosophy; cultural studies or cultural history; sociology; art history; American studies; drama; psychology; religious studies; modern languages; or music.

English also has a context outside of the academy. In the following sections we will therefore examine the importance of English in society and culture. In particular, you will find discussion of topics such as how the discipline contributes to the economy through the culture and tourism industries; what an English degree offers in terms of society and culture; and how skills learned on an English degree can specifically be applied to your future contribution to society.

How English contributes to the economy

English and English graduates contribute to the economy in myriad ways, but it is worth sometimes spelling this out as government and other organizations can underplay the role of the arts and humanities in wealth generation. We will touch on two areas here: the culture and creative industries and English's contribution to tourism.

Culture and creative industries

A review published by the British Academy, entitled 'That full complement of riches: the contributions of the arts, humanities and social sciences to the nation's wealth', quotes a Department for Culture, Media and Sport (DCMS) finding that the creative industries accounted for 5 per cent of Britain's GDP in 2001. The DCMS defines this industry as including television and radio, film and video, the performing arts and publishing. It is predicted that there will be a 136 per cent growth in output of the industries and a 46 per cent growth in employment from 1995 to 2015. The industries will become a larger employer of English graduates; already they employed 6.6 per cent of English leavers in 2004. What follows is a short introduction to the main culture and creative industries, and how they contribute to the economy.

The BBC began with radio in 1922, and is now accessed by millions worldwide; nearly 35 per cent of the viewing population watched one of the main BBC channels in 2004. Much programming involves dramatizations of existing literary works or the production of new material; the broadcast on Channel 4, in 1987, of Tony Harrison's poem 'V' is one such example of bringing new poetry to a mainstream audience. The programme caused great media controversy and debate especially amongst the tabloids, leading to a new edition containing the press coverage of the poem's screening. Not only do television and radio create revenue for the economy, they contribute to the richness of people's everyday lives and support the transmission of English studies through landmark programmes on language and literary adaptations that bring the classics to new audiences.

Cinema is another form of entertainment that generates considerable wealth. In 2001 there were over 141 million cinema visits, with high-grossing films including the adaptation of the popular children's *Harry Potter* books and J.R.R. Tolkien's *Lord of the Rings*. Literary adaptations of various kinds have become mainstream film fare, and a novel such as Bram Stoker's *Dracula* has been returned to repeatedly, with over 70 adaptations made for the screen between the 1920s and the 1990s. Alongside cinemas, a network of theatres exists countrywide, although they are most prolific in major cities, particularly the capital. The National Theatre, in London, opened in 1963 with a production of *Hamlet*. It now holds 1000 performances per year, and has 600,000 visitors.

Literary Festivals began in 1949, starting with the Cheltenham Literary Festival, which continues to attract many thousands of visitors for ten days every autumn. The Edinburgh International Festival focuses on the performing arts, aiming to showcase the best in Scottish culture to an international audience. Festivals are becoming more and more widespread, to attract millions of visitors drawn to different cultural areas, from music and film to fiction and poetry. Single-author festivals are increasingly common too, for example the Graham Greene Festival in his hometown of Berkhamstead.

Print media and publishing have evolved into a massive industry that digital technology is only likely to expand into new forms. The first British newspaper, *The London Gazette*, started in 1665, while magazines began to be produced in the following century.

Publishing thrived on a large scale in the nineteenth century, making many significant Victorian novelists accessible to a growing literate population. After World War Two, in a more competitive market for entertainment, Penguin began publishing their famous paperbacks in large numbers as prosperity and growing literacy brought more people to an appreciation of literature and culture. Now newspapers range from local to national, from tabloid to broadsheet; and magazines are available on almost every conceivable subject. With new digital technologies, newspapers, magazines and books are available via the internet, making them accessible on an even greater scale and creating more jobs in the culture sector. More broadly, it is clear that what we now call the creative industries both have a long history and will continue to contribute to the economy both in terms of investment and employment, providing opportunities for graduates of English studies as much as other disciplines.

The tourism industry

English-related industries not only add to the cultural fabric of the British population, they also contribute to the economy by stimulating tourism. For example, the number of tourists visiting Britain rose by 6 per cent between May 2005 and May 2006, from 29 million to nearly 31 million. Theatres and festivals, in particular, attract overseas visitors and therefore investment into the country.

Perhaps the most famous example of a small 'industry' growing around interest in a particular writer is that of Shakespeare and his hometown of Stratford, where he was born in 1564 and died in 1616. Today the town has three theatres, and a whole commercial infrastructure including restaurants, hotels and guesthouses, to cater for the tourist trade. This industry has created many jobs for local people. Another attraction to emerge from Shakespeare's fame is the reconstructed Globe Theatre in London, modelled on the theatre where Shakespeare worked, which was first constructed in 1599. The season runs from May to September, with Shakespeare's plays performed in a setting based on the original 'wooden O' (as Shakespeare calls the theatre in *Henry V*).

There are other areas of the country that attract visitors because of their literary associations. The Lake District, for example, is sometimes known as Wordsworth Country because of its link with the Romantic poet, William Wordsworth. His home, Dove Cottage, is now a museum and attracts 70 000 visitors a year. Hardy country, Jane Austen's regency Bath, Joyce's Dublin, and Laurie Lee's Cotswolds are all sites of pilgrimage and it is widely acknowledged today that a proportion of tourism's multi-billion-pound success is founded on the country's literary heritage.

In terms of language, English in its many varieties has clearly become dominant in many ways across the globe. Such influential institutions as the BBC, the UK Parliament and CNN have adopted the standard form of authorized 'correct' English; however, 'English' is much more widely spoken in the form of dialects, pidgins and creoles around the world. You will hear English in its many local styles in countries as diverse as Pakistan, Uganda, Jamaica and New Zealand. According to the latest estimates, around 1.3 billion people will be speaking a form of English by 2050, and the demand for specialist English language courses is set to rise six-fold by 2025, signalling that English is fast becoming the chief global language of business.

English subject knowledge and culture

On an English degree you not only study the literary or linguistic texts themselves, but are expected to learn about the contexts in which an author writes. This aspect of learning English contributes to an understanding of the development of British society and international relations.

Literature often also affects and contributes to our understanding of history. You may thus study texts composed as early as *Beowulf*, which was written in approximately AD 1000 in Anglo-Saxon, or Old English. This long poem gives important insights into the history of Anglo-Saxon culture: its myths and legends, as well as its politics. The text has been linked to a seventh-century ship-burial site at Sutton Hoo in Suffolk, as it gives insights into the Christian and Pagan practices of those that buried the ship. Here we see how literature may link with other disciplines; in this case archaeology (Sutton Hoo is also a crucial touchstone for Angus Wilson's much-admired 1956 comic novel *Anglo-Saxon Attitudes*). Associated with the knowledge gained of historical contexts is the understanding of how culture has both changed and remained similar. This enables students to see how the past was radically different as well as how it has influenced society today.

With regard to the significance of the study of language, one of the most important cultural changes within British society was the Great Vowel Shift. This phenomenon occurred between the fifteenth and eighteenth centuries and was characterized by the articulation of vowels higher up in the mouth, which signalled a huge alteration in how words are commonly pronounced. If you study Chaucer, you will know that he wrote in Middle English, in the fourteenth century, before the great vowel shift, and many of the rhymes in *The Canterbury Tales* no longer work because of the change.

'The past is a foreign country', L.P. Hartley says at the start of his novel *The Go-Between*, but English degrees today often introduce you to literature and language-use from a wide variety of nations and ethnicities. Studying English at university can provide a better appreciation of literature by non-canonical authors and minority cultures. For example, the novels of V.S. Naipaul (born in the Caribbean of Indian parentage) dissect the broad variety of modern experience in a post-colonial world, and texts such as *The Enigma of Arrival* also deal revealingly with the experience of migration within the UK through his unnamed main character's isolation and unrealized expectations. Another example would be Alan Hollinghurst, whose *The Swimming Pool Library* gives a candid account of gay culture in the 1980s, revisited in his Booker prize-winning novel *The Line of Beauty*. Similarly, the celebrated work of Jeanette Winterson and Sarah Waters has changed perceptions of lesbian experience among mainstream readers.

The English graduate's role in society

English students gain skills that can be applied to their chosen career, as well as on a personal level. These include disciplined reasoning, critical and analytical thinking, the ability to look at issues from a number of perspectives, and the development of greater creativity.

In terms of disciplined reasoning, an English degree gives you the opportunity to develop techniques of persuasion and argument, which can be applied to journalism, for instance, where you need to make concise points, supported by evidence. Through participating in seminars and doing presentations, studying English builds upon these abilities, including the political skill of debating – which can be used in both public speaking and private interactions. The use of rhetoric in speech-making can be a valuable asset alongside compelling evidence to substantiate your claims, and such devices as repetition to make strong points. Public speaking is of course a skill increasingly needed in a wide range of careers, and an English degree will help you to cultivate an appreciation of rhetoric, eloquence and persuasion.

English students also develop writing skills through assessment in a variety of formats. Essay writing involves the discussion of a set question, in which you are expected to show evidence of effective research from selected sources. Careers in management, in particular, demand these skills for the purpose of report writing. A good pre-sentation should contain succinct arguments and employ support-ing material such as handouts, as well as make use of IT provision, including PowerPoint if appropriate. These skills are particularly applicable to careers such as law, in which advocates must prepare presentations on a regular basis. In exams, students need to be pre-pared to submit a written argument under strictly timed conditions – this develops skills to assist time management and working under pressure. Careers such as marketing demand this type of skill, as it is a high-pressured business environment, where meeting tight dead-lines is essential. Note taking is a daily task on an English degree, in lectures and in the library, and involves a balance between the skills of listening, careful reading and writing. Such careers as arts adminis-tration need this skill, where employees are expected to take notes as well as contribute in meetings, and take accurate minutes.

English also fosters critical and analytical thought, which are needed in many careers, particularly those where finding both errors and shortcomings within documents is an essential pre-requisite. Administrative and management positions require this type of attention to detail and close reading skills are important in a range of careers where you need to draw independent and object-ive conclusions regarding the reliability of reports and accounts. Being able to analyse closely any form of text, whether it be in an employment or personal capacity, will contribute to your ability to make clear judgements in relation to the validity of any claim made by a writer.

As discussed in the previous chapter, literary theory is often taught as part of an English degree. The ability to examine a text from the diverse perspectives of these differing critical schools of thought (for instance Marxism, post-structuralism, post-colonialism, feminism and psychoanalysis) can also be used in encounters with other cultural forms, such as television, cinema, music and art, as well as novels, poetry and plays. With regard to these last-mentioned literary forms, many graduates pursue some form of creative writing, either as a pastime or at work. Within the suite of English studies, there are now creative writing courses running throughout the country, from diplomas in local colleges and community centres to Master's degrees at universities: the most famous of which is the MA in Creative Writing at the University of East Anglia.

The usefulness of cultivating creativity is not only limited to creative writing work, but can also be applied in careers such as advertising, where a high level of original and independent thought is required. More generally, the transferable skills acquired on an English degree allow graduates to benefit society and culture through habits of disciplined reflection as well as critical approaches to social questions approached as analytical problems or 'texts' from a number of perspectives. These skills are not just applicable to the workplace where graduates make an economic contribution to society, but also in everyday interactions with others.

In conclusion, English plays a vital public role in several ways: culturally through the study of a major world language and its written artefacts; economically through its considerable contribution to the creative and tourism industries; and societally through the subject knowledge and transferable skills gained by graduates. Which is to say that the study of English gives you the opportunity to benefit from language and literature's part in society and culture long after graduation.

Websites and further resources

General
www.intute.ac.uk/artsandhumanities/
An academic search engine that provides links to appropriate resources on the internet for English students.

English language
www.bbc.co.uk/radio4/routesofenglish

This website accompanies the Radio 4 programme 'Routes of English', which is an investigation into the history of the English language. There is information on each of the programmes, with the opportunity to listen again.

Crystal, D. (2003), *The Cambridge Encyclopaedia of the English Language*, 2nd edn. Cambridge: Cambridge University Press. A useful reference book on all aspects of the English language. This second edition includes the addition of new information on world English and internet English.

Crystal, D. (2004), *The Stories of English*. London: Penguin. A comprehensive history of the English language from its beginnings up to the present day, with a particular focus on non-standard forms.

English literature

Medieval, Renaissance and seventeenth century
www.luminarium.org/lumina.htm

A website devoted to the above periods in English literature, through which information on prominent authors and historical contexts of the periods can be found, as well as a selection of academic essays.

Romantic
www.rc.umd.edu/

This website is an extensive guide devoted to romantic literature and culture. It has a 'Scholarly Resources' section, which provides useful bibliographies for further research.

Nineteenth century
www.victorianweb.org/

A comprehensive guide to political, social history, gender, science, religion and philosophy of the time. In addition, a list of the most important authors through which information on their lives and works can be found.

Contemporary and postcolonial literature
www.contemporarywriters.com

This website, run by the British Council, contains a database of British and Commonwealth authors, where biographies, bibliographies, criticism, prizes and photographs can be searched and browsed easily.

www.usp.nus.edu.sg/landow/post/

This website contains brief and concise information on authors and their country of origin, covering Africa, Australia, New Zealand, South Asia, Singapore, Canada, the Caribbean, UK and Ireland.

Drabble, M. (ed.) (2000), *The Oxford Companion to English Literature*. Oxford: Oxford University Press. An excellent reference guide to authors, books, literary theory, allusions and characters, which can form a sound basis for further research or simple clarification.

Creative writing

Anderson, L. (2005), *Creative Writing: A Workbook with Readings*. London: Routledge. A practical guide to creative writing, which includes exercises to develop skills. Suitable for students as well as individuals interested in doing creative writing as a hobby.

4 English and employment

As has been said, English is sometimes considered a 'non-vocational' subject but you will find it more helpful to consider it multi-vocational. This should be taken to mean that it is a subject most students decide to take without a particular career in mind. When choosing English, many students will not be considering any definite area of employment after their degree and will rightly see the study of literature and language as an end in itself.

However, you will probably proceed to some form of paid work after you finish your degree, although this may be preceded by further study or by other non-paid activities. It is helpful, therefore, to reflect on the kinds of employment English graduates commonly choose, and some of the skills required by those jobs or professions. First, we may say that in addition to the literary and linguistic content itself, the most significant subject-specific knowledge and skills English students acquire centre on: the contexts of literature (historical, intellectual and cultural); close reading abilities; knowledge of diverse theoretical and critical approaches (the areas where lecturers are least satisfied with student attainment). According to surveys, the most important general skills English cultivates in addition to subject-specific ones are: self-reflection and self-criticism; mental flexibility; critical reasoning; conceptual and analytical skills; communication skills and creativity (conversely, the degree is not thought likely to promote your enterprise and negotiation skills).

With these skills in mind, in this chapter we look at the opportunities available to English students, suggesting some non-traditional and unexpected career destinations as well as well-trodden paths.[1] English is a diverse and versatile discipline, and will prepare you for a wide variety of careers, some of which may not seem obvious.[2] Here you will find an exploration of some of the options, comment on how past students have used their degree, and advice on where to find information on careers, including part-time employment, voluntary work and work experience whilst studying. You will also find other choices, if you do not wish to proceed to a career immediately, such as postgraduate study.

As previously said, English studies is traditionally seen as an academic degree. However, in many respects it is really poly-vocational, so employment opportunities are very broad.[3] Careers available are as varied as advertising and marketing, teaching, pub-lishing and media work as well as less apparent alternatives, such as law.[4] What follows are some examples of career choices as well as the duties and training requirements they involve.

Teaching

If you wish to use your subject knowledge directly then teaching may be an appropriate career choice. The Teacher Training Agency (TTA) advises that this vocation is particularly appealing for gradu-ates who are interested in and inspired by children or adolescents, and who wish to encourage them to engage with and enjoy the study of English.[5] It is a career that requires dedication, patience and creativity as it is both physically and intellectually challenging. There are decisions to be made regarding which age group to teach, with the options of primary or secondary schools as well as post-16 further education. Whichever age range you choose, you will be required to undertake a Postgraduate Certificate of Education, or PGCE, or a PGCFE in the case of further education. This training involves a one-year intensive course, taken after completing your undergraduate degree. The prospect of motivating a class of 30 young people may seem daunting but, as the TTA says, teachers encourage children to learn and foster what can become a much longer-term pursuit, which most will testify is an extremely reward-ing aspect of the job.[6]

Commercial

Some graduates would prefer to work in either an office or retail environment, making the publishing or bookselling industries more appealing opportunities than teaching. A publishing career is most commonly entered through the post of publishing assistant; however, after gaining experience in this role, there is the possibility of pro-gressing to desk editor then to commissioning editor.[7] Alter-natively, there is the option of working freelance as a publishing copy-editor and proofreader.[8] The role of a commissioning editor is to generate new titles for publishers' portfolios, and you will be responsible for investigating which titles are most popular with con-sumers, liaising with writers and managing other staff members. This career is attainable with a minimum of five years' experience of working within the publishing industry; a postgraduate qualifica-tion such as an MA in publishing may be of assistance.

Copy-editors and proofreaders work on contractual terms with publishers, which means usually working at home; the primary role is to ensure books are clear to the reader and accurate in terms of such aspects as punctuation. After gaining considerable work experience, you might progress to lead responsibility for a complete book, from its conception to publication. Again there are post-graduate qualifications that would assist you in pursuing this career, but your English degree would be beneficial for these avenues because the degree is evidence of training in critical and analytical skills.

Another aspect of the industry is the promotion, marketing and selling of the books themselves, which often provides opportunities to meet the public face to face on a daily basis. You would need to be a sound communicator, well organized and in possession of a broad understanding of a range of subject matter – all attributes fostered through the study of English.[9] The main job-related tasks include helping customers by giving them information about books they may wish to purchase, sometimes using computer databases and operating till systems. There is also the opportunity to assist with book-related events, such as book signings and poetry readings. Bookselling is an exciting area of retail to become involved in, and will give you the opportunity to use your initiative more than other retail sectors would, for example in terms of responsibility for buying stock and budget management.

Librarianship

Librarianship also gives you the opportunity to meet and assist others, whether you are employed in an academic or a public capacity. Academic librarians generally work in universities, further education or research institutes and may be involved in some teaching activities in relation to the use of research methods and information tools in a learning environment.[10] Within this branch of the profession you would also have the chance to apply specific subject knowledge through specializing in English.

Public librarians are mainly employed by local authorities and provide a service to the surrounding community.[11] Increasingly, librarians are expected to have a sound grasp of information technology, particularly the use of the internet and associated resources. Most librarians begin their careers as library assistants, while completing the postgraduate qualifications necessary to become fully qualified; this training could take the form of either a Postgraduate Diploma or a Master's Degree in librarianship, information science or information management. Whichever route you choose, librarianship offers an intellectually challenging career and makes good use of English skills.

Journalism

Another popular option for English graduates is journalism, which may be of particular interest to you if you find the element of writing in your degree to be the most enjoyable. Journalists work in two main sectors: broadcast and print. Broadcast journalists are engaged in radio and television and are, according to June Kay, involved in initiating ideas for stories and researching them, which might include talking to relevant parties involved, then generating an article suitable for the intended audience.[12] Print journalists are employed to do a similar job, but in a different medium: newspapers, magazines or journals. In order to enter either sector of the profession a postgraduate qualification is almost essential, as well as having some form of prior experience.[13] This career is also very competitive and undertaking a related work placement during vacations, or assisting on a university newspaper, would be beneficial.

Law

Law may seem a less obvious career to choose, but is an excellent profession to enter for more than a few English graduates. Barristers tend to work in Crown and Higher Courts providing advocacy, from cases brought against alleged criminals, to multinational corporations, to complex divorce proceedings; solicitors are now working increasingly in higher courts, such as Crown Courts, due to a decrease in restrictions.[14] To enable you to work in law as an English graduate – as either a barrister or solicitor – you would need to take a postgraduate conversion course called a Common Professional Examination (CPE) or a Graduate Diploma in Law (GDL).[15] For those wishing to pursue careers as a barrister, a further qualification known as a Bar Vocational Course is necessary. Whichever path you decide upon, a career in law frequently involves conveying an argument convincingly through public speaking, so it is a sound option for those who are confident debaters in seminar situations and who enjoy giving presentations.

This is by no means an exhaustive list of opportunities for you to choose from on completion of your degree in English. Most companies that recruit graduates do not require a specific subject because the fact that someone has studied successfully for a degree is taken as evidence of intellectual ability.

English employment destinations

Evidence of the employability of English graduates is strong, both in terms of employment rates and the career patterns of previous students. A 'Prospects' national survey of graduates finishing their degree in 2003, which included 83.1 per cent of all English graduates, found that over half were in employment in the UK, while others were either studying for further qualifications or overseas; only 6.3 per cent were believed to be unemployed.[16] Of those that were employed, 19.6 per cent were in administrative or secretarial roles, 13.8 per cent in teaching, 11.4 per cent were commercial, industrial or public sector managers, 6.8 per cent were in health and childcare related professions, and 6.2 per cent were in media, public relations, literary, design or sports professions. What this data shows most obviously is the breadth of careers for which an English degree will prepare you.

However, these statistics were collected soon after students graduated; a CHERI survey carried out several years after students finished university gives a clearer indication of longer-term career patterns.[17] Through this survey it was found that only 9 per cent of English graduates had experienced unemployment during the time period, which is a similar percentage rate to that for all university leavers. However, it was found that most English graduates were working in either the public or non-profit making sectors. Overall, 84 per cent were in jobs expected to be taken by graduates, showing that those with an English degree are very capable of maintaining employment at the same level as other graduates and underlining how a multi-vocational subject such as English can prove beneficial in terms of your career choice after graduation without preparing you for one profession alone.[18]

Careers information

To provide you with the best information about employment opportunities as well as offer guidance while you are studying, all colleges and universities run careers services. These support units will include resources such as reference books, informative literature on career opportunities, and the latest graduate vacancies; in addition there will be careers advisors who are available to assist with your planning after graduation.[19] There are likely also to be careers events within institutions, at which you can meet prospective employers, both local and national. Also there are countrywide events of a similar kind, although on a larger scale, held for example at Birmingham's National Exhibition Centre – universities often organize trips to such events. The internet is also a source of information and advice for students, particularly the Prospects website at www.prospects.ac.uk, which is specifically designed to assist graduates with career planning and also provides details of vacancies.

Work experience

Work experience can be voluntary or paid employment and involves any job undertaken before embarking on your career. As well as part-time or voluntary work, this could take the form of 'work shadowing', which is when a student watches an employee at work in order to gain insight into his or her job. Sources of information about work experience include: the Prospects website and magazine;

university careers centres; and the National Council for Work Experience (www.work-experience.org), with its own guide specifically for students. In addition they give details of organizations that operate schemes. Applications for such placements should be made formally, and in the same way as if you were applying for a full-time job because there is much competition when vacancies arise. Work experience is beneficial because it enables you to gain new skills and decide on a specific career. It will also be impressive to future prospective employers when you are looking for employment after graduation.[20]

Voluntary work

Volunteering can be part of work experience gained while studying. It is particularly beneficial when applying for careers in areas such as social work and teaching, as a means of demonstrating suitable skills, prior commitment and an understanding of the profession's demands.[21] The Prospects' website advises that voluntary work need not interfere with your studies, as only a morning or an afternoon per week is sufficient to gain insight into a profession, develop relevant skills and demonstrate capability to the appropriate agencies.

Student Community Action, which is run as part of universities' student unions, often run a number of volunteering projects from working with children to assisting adults with disabilities or the elderly. There may also be the opportunity to form your own project, as all such initiatives are student led. Participating in a scheme such as this enables you to gain valuable work experience and also make a contribution to the local community. Voluntary work of this kind is specifically relevant for English students because of the numbers who enter either the public or non-profit making sectors once they graduate.[22]

Advice for students who are unsure about which career to choose

When beginning an English degree not everybody has a specific career in mind, which is where voluntary work or work experience can be of great assistance. Many students choose English studies because of an enthusiasm for and interest in literature, language or creative writing, and wish to devote their time to the degree without planning for post-university employment. However, some thought does need to be given to the future, daunting though it may sometimes seem. A good place to start is with an objective consideration of your attributes – both positive and negative – as well as the skills you are developing through both studying and part-time work. These could be listed with the relevant examples, and become a starting point for thinking about possible careers.

A further means of exploring career options is the internet tool, Prospects Planner, on the Prospects website.[23] Once registered on this, students are asked to answer a series of questions relating to skills, attributes and preferences; a series of career options are then given, which can be further investigated. Similar tools may be available at university career centres. They can be an effective basis for career planning if students are unsure of the type of employment that might suit them.

Postgraduate study

Postgraduate study is an interesting alternative if you find your undergraduate course in English particularly enjoyable. Taught Master's (MA) courses in literature, language or creative writing are run at universities throughout the UK. The variety of specialisms is immense, with courses ranging from Middle English to European literature. There is also the opportunity to study in another area that may relate to English, or on a vocational course, such as those required for librarianship or journalism. According to a UK Graduate Careers Survey in 2003, postgraduate courses are becoming increasingly popular, with more graduates embarking upon them than going straight into employment.[24] Gaining funding can be difficult however; the Arts and Humanities Research Council (AHRC) has grant awards for taught Master's degrees as well as Research degrees, but there is the option of combining part-time work with study if no award can be secured. Therefore, you should think carefully through your decision to embark upon a postgraduate qualification, taking into consideration issues such as finance and time management as well as choice of subject, before applying.[25]

An English degree equips you with the necessary knowledge and skills to enter a diverse range of professions, giving prospective employers a strong indication of your abilities and aptitude. As a graduate you can expect to enter a career that will both challenge and interest you, building on many of the skills developed in your time as an English student.

Websites and further resources

General careers

Jenner, Shirley (2000), *The Graduate Career Handbook: Make the Right Start for a Bright Future*. London Pearson Education. A comprehensive guide to careers for all graduates that gives advice on the whole process of career planning, from deciding which career to pursue to beginning employment.

www.prospects.ac.uk

The most comprehensive careers website with facilities ranging from the means to find a suitable career if you are undecided, to the latest graduate vacancies. Prospects publish a number of career-related magazines, some on specific career sectors, such as *Focus on Law*, and others on postgraduate opportunities (including *Postgrad Magazine*) and *Prospects Finalist*, which gives general information to graduating students. These should be found at universities' careers centres.

Swann, Jamie (ed.) (2004) *AgCAS Special Interest Series*. Sheffield: AgCAS. A series of booklets that give succinct and useful advice on career-related topics from interview techniques to continuing study.

English careers

Dixon, Beryl (2002), *What can I do with an Arts Degree?* Richmond: Trotman and Company. There is a specific section dedicated to English within this book, where the emphasis is on less traditional career choices.

Career specific

Tatterton, Jane (ed.) 2003, *AgCAS Sector Briefings*, Sheffield: AgCAS. A series of booklets, each dedicated to a specific career sector, for example publishing, education and legal, which includes information about the career as well as case studies and further resources.

Journalism
www.bbc.co.uk/jobs/

A comprehensive site for anyone interested in applying for employment with the BBC, including work experience opportunities.

Law
www.lcan.org.uk

This is the website for the Law Careers Advice Network, giving information on training and recruitment statistics, as well as links to websites which contain vacancies for vacation placements and mini-pupillages.

Teaching
www.teach.gov.uk

A website designed to give advice on such matters as training requirements and finding employment in the profession, as well as giving an insight into the demands of the career.

PART TWO: Key skills

In this part of the book, we will look at the essential study skills for English: reading, writing, research, note-taking and revision for exams. These are the core skills that will inform, and to an extent determine, the level of success you achieve on your course. Together with your acquisition of greater knowledge and understanding, and your enjoyment of the course itself, the development of key skills is the most important part of your study in higher education. Key skills are the ones that will help you succeed at degree level but they are also extremely important for your future employment prospects. Advanced and sophisticated literacy skills, together with the ability to work independently on tasks assigned to you, or developed through your own initiative, form the core around which many jobs are built, as discussed in Part One. While the subject knowledge acquired on many degrees, including English, is of direct use in a limited number of employment situations, both the core and transferable skills cultivated on your course will be ones in which nearly all employers are interested.

In terms of tools to assist you in connecting up the skill-set you develop at university or college with your planning for employment, a government initiative outlined in the 2003 White Paper, *The Future of Higher Education*, has introduced the concept of a personal development plan/portfolio (PDP) with the objective of helping you to understand your own learning patterns, and to use this skill to plan for your future.[1] In the twenty-first century, students will be increasingly expected to reflect upon their own intellectual development, and this process should begin in school, progress through further and higher education and continue throughout employment post-graduation. PDPs, together with your transcripts of course results and achievements, are sometimes referred to as progress files, which are meant to encourage you to examine your skills and build into an invaluable tool to support you in compiling a CV (Curriculum Vitae) when making job applications.

A CV is the standard means of showing your suitability for a specific type of employment in a concise and coherent manner.[2] It needs to include an employment aim or aspiration that you can express as the motivation for your job application, as well as details of previous and current education, employment and, if appropriate, other activities such as hobbies. Although it is best to start writing your CV as early as possible, when graduation approaches and you are beginning to think more deeply about employment after university, your institution's careers advisors should be able to assist with compiling an effective CV. It will be helpful as you move through the levels of your degree to keep a record of such things as vacation work and the skills it has involved, so that the necessary information to compile your CV is always at hand.

It may also be necessary for you to have a CV while at university because increasingly, and particularly with the rise in tuition fees and undergraduate debt, students need to undertake some form of part-time employment while studying. This may be in vacations, but is more often in term-time, in order to meet the financial burdens that now exist, including rent, bills and fees. A MORI Poll, which surveyed 1103 students across 22 universities in 2001, asked the question 'Have you done or are you doing any of the following types of work during your years at university?' It found 30 per cent of students were working between one and 29 hours per week during term time while nearly 2 per cent were doing more than 30 hours.[3] A further 20 per cent were undertaking some kind of work during university vacations.

If you become one of the growing number of students that does need to work during your time at university, there are many sources of assistance in finding part-time employment. A national web-based employment agency called www.hotrecruit.co.uk assists students in finding suitable jobs within their local area. Local press publications also often have an employment section where jobs are advertised. Another means of finding more flexible work is to join local recruitment agencies, which can assist with fitting work around your studies as they offer mainly temporary contracts. Increasingly, student unions have a job shop scheme, offering help with finding part-time work, and giving details of suitable current vacancies. However, most universities would advise that part-time work should be restricted to a minimum, particularly during term-time, because there is a risk that it could begin to impinge upon your studies. This warning is particularly pertinent to English studies where, as we have said, there is an expectation that you will read widely as part of your degree, and it is with reading that we will now begin a review of core skills in English studies.

Further reading on CVs and PDPs

Bright, Jim and Earl, Joanne (2001), *Brilliant CV: What Employers Want to See and How to Say It*. London: Pearson Education Ltd. This book is a very useful and clear guide to writing successful curricula vitae, with lots of examples to assist students and graduates.

Cottrell, Stella (2003), *Skills for Success: The Personal Development Planning Handbook*. Basingstoke: Palgrave Macmillan. This book gives very practical advice on personal development planning, including exercises to assist with the process.

5 Reading

> The focussed discussion of reading lies at the heart of learning in the subject. It is important that students are able to engage in dialogue, and develop and negotiate conclusions with others, which is a key component in the acquisition of both subject-specific and transferable skills.
>
> (English Benchmarking Statement)

On all English studies modules, the methods of teaching, learning and assessment are given careful consideration and are informed by clear aims and expectations. You will soon find that classes employ a range of learning methods, often incorporating aspects of independent learning such as project or group work and worksheets. These elements are designed to give you the opportunity to engage actively with the material under study, to stimulate your intellectual curiosity and to elicit a lively response to primary and secondary sources. Like the principles of personal development planning, a structured and supported programme of independent learning within a module will always be designed to provide an opportunity for you to give some reflective thought to your own learning, as well as improve your analytical and problem-solving skills.

English is a highly textual field of study and demands intensive reading. Indeed, you should see reading and not lectures as the main source of stimulation, if not inspiration. Lecturers will often deliberately open out discussion and encourage you to investigate a subject independently and you should ensure that you make full use of library or Learning Centre resources, particularly of the journal holdings, which can be a source for cutting-edge or radical critical readings. Most English modules are structured around specific texts. These texts may be novels, short stories, poems or plays, but they may be also be, for example, essays of literary criticism, theory, or abstract arguments which deal with methods and strategies of writing or reading.

Also, apart from the required primary reading, a number of additional critical texts may be recommended and these will provide valuable help in the understanding and interpretation of the prescribed texts. However, this recommended secondary reading might not necessarily be a direct commentary on a primary text or even an author. It could be on the cultural or literary movement of which the text or the author in question is a part. For example, if your required reading is James Joyce's *A Portrait of the Artist as a Young Man* (1916), the recommended reading could well be on Modernism in general, or Irish politics, or Irish literature, or themes such as gender relations, colonialism, or aesthetic philosophy. It is not uncommon for recommended reading to be of a theoretical nature, which is intended to provide varied tools and strategies for the analysis of primary texts.

How and how much?

Where pre-university study usually involves the detailed scrutiny of a small number of set books, English at university moves quickly through a comparatively large number of primary texts. Consequently, a 2004 report asked students, among many other things, how well prepared they felt for the range and quantity of primary and secondary reading required in HE, and for placing texts in historical and social contexts.[1] The results of the survey overall showed that students felt less well-prepared for this aspect of English studies than any other. Indeed, only 22 per cent of the students surveyed felt they were suitably prepared for the amount of reading of primary texts (novels, plays, poems, linguistic texts and so on) they were required to do, while a third considered they were poorly prepared. A quarter felt well prepared for the amount of secondary reading (critical, historical and theoretical texts), and 28 per cent felt poorly prepared. Those who had studied A-level English literature (rather than a language and literature course or an access course, for example) were slightly more likely to say they felt well prepared. In terms of putting texts in historical, literary, or social context, 30 per cent felt well prepared and 24 per cent poorly prepared for this aspect of their studies.

Who and what?

English literature is one of those subjects that are defined more from within than without. By this we mean that its object is not just more cultural than natural, for example like a social science such as economics or sociology, but is almost entirely cultural. Many subjects debate their parameters but a disciplinary area such as English literature even debates whether it has a central object of study. Is there a 'canon' of English literature? Where did it come from? Who decided what was in and what was out? Should there be a canon?

Tom Stoppard, in his play *The Real Thing*, has a central character argue to her playwright husband: 'You judge everything as though everyone starts from the same place, aiming at the same prize: Eng. Lit. Shakespeare out there in front by a mile and the rest of the field strung out behind trying to close the gap.'

The playwright replies by digging out his cricket bat and saying:

> This thing here, which looks like a wooden club, is actually several pieces of particular wood cunningly put together in a certain way so the whole thing is sprung, like a dance floor. It's for hitting cricket balls with. If you get it right, the cricket ball will travel two hundred yards in four seconds, and all you've done is give it a knock like knocking the top off a bottle . . . What we're trying to do is write cricket bats, so that when we throw up an idea and give it a little knock, it might . . . travel . . .

The suggestion here is that some writing *works* better than other writing: is both better made and more successful because its ideas resonate. This is highly contentious, yet it is generally true that for those who study 'Eng. Lit.' there is a changing but broadly stable hierarchy of writers, one end of which is identified in the simple division between those writers who are included on the syllabus and those who are not. In terms of what is taught (as opposed to read or researched), this is how the subject is defined from within, even though there are many voices without that influence the choices made.

The idea of a literary canon derives from the term's use in the Catholic Church where the 'canon' refers to those texts considered to be divine scripture. The notion of authentic and authoritative texts was later applied to language and classical studies, where there were disputes over authorship, originality, corruption and forgery. It is a short step from this debate over a text's worth centred on authenticity to one focused on value: aesthetic, cultural, formal and artistic. A hierarchy of poetry and to a lesser extent of poetic forms has been in place for many centuries, while fiction has been separated into genre(s) and 'literature'. When a piece of writing becomes 'literature' it curiously loses its genre tag – *Brave New World, Frankenstein* and *The Lord of the Flies* are all books that could be, but are not, located in genre fiction (science fiction, horror, children's literature, for example).

What and who students are asked to read will vary from one institution to another and between choices made within the programme offered. In terms of single-author modules likely to be encountered, the following list of writers covers most of those currently studied on English literature courses:[2] Jane Austen; Samuel Beckett; William Blake; the Brontës; Lord Byron; Angela Carter; Joseph Conrad; Charles Dickens; John Donne; George Eliot; Thomas Hardy; Henry James; James Joyce; Ben Jonson; Rudyard Kipling; D.H. Lawrence; Philip Larkin; Andrew Marvell; John Milton; V.S. Naipaul; Sylvia Plath; Edmund Spenser; Jonathan Swift; Oscar Wilde; and W.B. Yeats. Of these, only Naipaul is still living, while Beckett, Yeats and Kipling have also won the Nobel Prize for Literature, along with T.S. Eliot, Harold Pinter, Doris Lessing and William Golding, who do not figure in this list. Who is taught is a question of which kinds of writing are valued, and what for. With contemporary writers, recurrent inclusion on a syllabus is less predictable than with those from before the twentieth century and few authors from the last 50 years are secure in the canon of taught writers.

On, around and off the syllabus

One of the most significant changes in study habits you will probably encounter in higher education concerns the amount of studying you are expected to do around the syllabus in addition to reading and re-reading the primary texts. To an extent, the primary text you will be asked to read forms the first dialogue you need to have in order to be able to enter into other dialogues; a second will be with staff and students; a third will be with critics who have commented on the text and the author; a fourth will be with commentators who have written about the literary, cultural, social, political and historical contexts for the primary text. This sounds like a great deal of course, and you are not expected to engage with everything, but the more you read the more you are likely to be able to contextualize your own initial response to reading the primary text. As you progress through the levels of your study it is likely you will do more and more secondary or contextual reading. It is also probable that a further element of your reading – theory – will grow, as you increasingly seek to situate your reading of the text into a structured argument consciously informed by a particular perspective.

We looked above at the most commonly taught authors, and the first kind of reading 'off the syllabus' that you might usefully undertake is of other key literary texts and authors. There is no single text that you will be expected to read on each and every English studies degree – a surprising fact perhaps – but there are many authors whose work it will be of benefit to you to be familiar with, including Chaucer, Shakespeare, Milton, Wordsworth, Joyce, Yeats, Woolf, Austen, Orwell, Donne, Blake, George Eliot, the Brontës, Hardy, Dickens, Conrad, T.S. Eliot and Samuel Beckett. This list is to an extent arbitrary but as a suggestion of up to 20 authors whose work is most referenced in the mainstream of English studies, it would not be wide of the mark. You may want to create your own 'canon' of key authors to reflect the emphases of your own degree course, or you might want to think of an alternative list of non-canonical authors who, for example, reflect a better mix of gender and ethnicity. Such an exercise would help you to consider the merits of different units or modules you undertake: why particular authors and texts have been selected is a question worth asking, but do not jump to easy conclusions: the texts are unlikely to have been chosen because they are the lecturer's preferences/favourites, or simply because they are canonical, or because they are 'teacherly' (a phrase meaning different things to different people, but suggesting that they are texts that generate discussion), but all these will be factors, as will the broader institutional context of the module and of English studies itself. There are wide differences between the texts taught on different English courses in the UK, but there are also many similarities and you may want to review the points made in relation to the English benchmark statement in the first chapter.

The next key area is critical vocabulary. Along with a good dictionary and thesaurus, you will want to have access to a guide on literary terminology. Like all specialisms, English studies has a vocabulary of its own, and many familiar terms will have different nuances while many unfamiliar terms will have complex or disputed meanings. How confident, for example, are you that you know what is meant by terms such as irony, realism, gender, post-modernism, deconstruction or the uncanny? This vocabulary also ranges from literary critical terms to theoretical concepts, and you will find it helpful to have an understanding of each.

The other area to think about is contextual reading. Literary historical knowledge is obviously helpful to you but so is cultural, political and social understanding – this may indeed be more helpful to you depending on your course of study and the emphases of particular modules or units. Clearly, this is where issues of time management and life priorities come into question. You need to work out for yourself how important it is to read different texts that are on, around and off the syllabus. This will depend on your reasons for doing the course to begin with. For example, do they include these: to get the best degree result; to get into a particular profession; to go on to further study; to develop your subject knowledge and understanding in a suitably conducive educational environment; or to broaden your interests? It may be that your reasons involve a combination of a large number of elements, but the reading you choose to do will follow on from such motivations. Consequently, you may want to read for pleasure, for edification, or solely for the purposes of assessment. Above all, try to remember that English studies should be enjoyable and, although it is a stock phrase to use, it is nonetheless true that you will get out of the degree what you put in. And what you put in will primarily be reading and thinking about the texts you read.

Please see the chapter 'Further reading and resources', for examples of texts you might buy or consult, but ensure you also learn to exercise judgement in your use of secondary material. Read critics critically and remember the fact that because someone has published a book or an article does not mean that they have pronounced the last word on a given subject. This is even more of an issue when using internet sources. You may want to quote a critic to support your own thinking, but you may also wish to argue against a particular critic's point of view. In either case you should never feel intimidated by critics: their writings are valuable contributions to the community of learning (of which you are also a part) and you should learn to read them with the same discriminating eye that you bring to primary texts.[3]

Skimming, reading, relevance

With all this material available to you, how should you decide what to read and how should you read it when you have decided? In answer to the first question, you do need to remember the old adage that there is no right answer in English studies. Markers value creativity, originality, flair, argument and idiosyncratic but cogent analysis. Having said this, there are answers that reflect the critical consensus and then there are 'riskier answers': ones that rely solely on your own personal response to the text; ones that assess the characters as though they are real people; ones that rely on understanding the text through the author's biography; ones that address the question tangentially; ones that have an unusual structure or take a formulaic approach to arranging the material. Reading helps to avoid these 'riskier answers' because it provides you with more knowledge and understanding. In general terms, we can say that, first, the more relevant reading is to the question you have been set the more directly helpful it will be; second, the more relevant it is to the angle your answer is going to take the more you will probably benefit; and, third, the more relevant to the text under discussion the better (although some people work best by reading unrelated material and transferring or applying ideas). When considering this, make sure you remember that 'the question' will have several terms within it and therefore several dimensions – do not lightly neglect some in favour of others. Also, the reading most obviously relevant to the question will be the reading that the majority of students are likely to want to undertake, so remember two more things: relying on the most obvious reading to inform your answer is quite likely to lead to an average grade; and the best texts you can read to write engagingly for the marker are unlikely to be found in the most obvious places, unless you have been specifically directed to them by the question-setter. Also, think about that word 'relevance': it is not one that markers often take kindly to because it is overused. Relevance can sometimes be a euphemism for 'easy to connect with' or 'readily comprehended'. The most intriguing work frequently occurs when the writer, whether an academic critic or a student, makes new links and undertakes fresh analyses by success-fully revealing or re-imagining what is 'relevant'.

In consideration of the second question above, remember that you don't have to undertake research by scouring each book (or other source) you have selected for secondary reading from cover to cover. First, use the contents page to inform your decision. Second, consult the index and look for key words. Third, be guided by the recommendations of others: tutors, fellow students, other sources and critics. You are often best advised to skim through a book to try to see what is most relevant to your assignment and what is less so. This does not mean that you should 'skip'; it means you should use the time available to you in the best way possible. If you read more thoughtfully rather than more passively, you will be better able to sift and select between and within texts; which is to say that reading is a process which can be vigorous in the sense of an active engagement with the words on the page in an energetic dialogue between the text and the reader, or can be active in the sense that the reader draws on a multitude of opinions and forms a range of new thoughts from consulting, skimming, and scrutinizing a variety of texts in many forms and in different ways at varying speeds.

6 Research[1]

You will probably have taken notes from books before. When you start studying at university you may therefore think of books as the main library resource for your degree work. However, there are other sources for productive inquiry and in this chapter we will look at some of the ways and means by which research is conducted by English students in higher education.

Journals

What are journals?

Journals are periodic publications, often released quarterly. They carry articles covering the latest research within a particular subject area, and may relate to a specific genre, period or approach. The articles are scholarly and often complex, but can be key or even essential reading to assist with your research at undergraduate level. They should be consulted as part of your routine work for assignments, particularly at levels 2 and 3.

What journals are there?

There are two main forms of periodical that can be found and used for research purposes. In terms of academic journals, all university and college libraries will have a reading list of the ones that they hold for a particular subject discipline. It is good practice to obtain a copy of this as soon as possible and consult it for each assignment set. For example, for an essay question such as 'Discuss the role of nature in romantic poetry', you may find useful the period journal *Eighteenth-century Studies* or the genre-specific journal *Romanticism*. There will also be multi-disciplinary or cross-disciplinary journals that prove useful in assisting with research for a particular assignment.

Additionally, high-quality papers such as the *Guardian* or the *Independent* carry book reviews and cultural discussions, which contain articles on new publications as well as author interviews that can prove useful and help you to keep abreast of current popular titles on a particular subject. In-depth articles can be also found in publications such as the *Times Literary Supplement* and the *London Review of Books*. These are all more frequent publications than academic journals.

How can I access journals?

As already mentioned, universities hold an A to Z listing of all journals that are stocked in their libraries/LRCs. This list is often available on your university's website, and is a good starting point for finding relevant journal articles. Librarians are available to assist should you have difficulty accessing this list.

However, looking on library shelves for relevant journal articles can be a time-consuming process, and it is often much easier to consult online indexes. You will probably be shown how to use these when you first arrive at university. Online indexes include the British Humanities Index, Humanities Abstracts, Index to Theses, ISI Web of Knowledge and the *Times Literary Supplement*. All of these indexes are useful for all English students so you would be wise to familiarize yourself with them early on. They contain lists of journal articles, with descriptions of their content, which can be found using the search tool facilities too. Often they are linked to the university library's website, so availability of articles found can also be checked. Like books that are unavailable within the library, journal articles can also be ordered through the inter-library loan service.

When utilizing these databases it is important to be able to search effectively. Although help is always available, regular use will enhance your searching skills. It is often advisable when searching one of these databases to use keywords from the essay title; so, from the above example, it may prove useful to begin with a search under the terms 'nature' and 'Romanticism'. Alternatively, you might choose to search under the names of authors or texts to be used in the essay, for example 'Wordsworth' and '*Prelude*' for the above title.

In the case of the British Humanities Index it is possible to search under the following categories: key words, author of article, title of article and descriptors (short contents within an article). When searching for 'Romanticism' and 'nature' under the criteria 'descriptors' the article 'In city pent: echo and allusion in Wordsworth, Coleridge and Lamb, 1797–1801' by Lucy Newlyn (*Review of English Studies*, 32, November 1981, pp. 408–428) was found. The experimentation with different key words and search terms will either widen a search or make a search more specific.

There are also online journals available, many of which can often be located through your university's library website. For the above question, there is the online journal *Romanticism (Edinburgh)*, which can be found on the host site Humanities International Complete. Once connected to the host site it is possible to do an advanced search for articles in the same way as searching for an article in an index. In the case of online journals, though, it is often possible to see the full article in PDF format. It is essential to use these tools regularly in order to find suitable articles both for general reading and assignments.

What should I look for in a journal?
Similar questions of journals need to be asked of books when examining whether an article is suitable for use in an assignment. Most important, perhaps, is to ask how relevant the article is to an assignment. However, journals can often prove most useful for contextualizing a question or giving background information about a period or genre. Also it is important to look for different arguments or opinions surrounding a question, for example in the above question it may be interesting to examine it in terms of eco-criticism or from a post-structuralist viewpoint. Careful use of journals in these ways will assist in effective research and add greatly to your understanding of current thinking on a particular topic or question.

The internet

The world wide web has become a popular source of information for students, but it must be used carefully and with a critical eye. Many sites are not appropriate sources for degree-level assignments, and over-dependence on such material will be penalized when work is assessed. What is very important when using the web, however, is that this material *must* be referenced in the same way as a book or a journal article. Articles and other work published on websites have authors, titles and addresses, and, even where these are not obvious, as full a reference as possible should be given whenever you use such sources, whether you are quoting directly, paraphrasing or using an idea suggested by a source on the web.

What internet resources are there?

There are numerous resources available to English students on the internet that will assist you with research, be it for general reading or specifically for an assignment. There are six main types of website that may prove to be of most use to students of English: author-specific, genre-specific, historical, bibliographic, books online, and journals/newspapers online.

Author-specific websites contain useful critical evaluations of a specific writer; this may include biographical information, critical appraisals of and examples of their work. This material is of course particularly useful in terms of gaining valuable information on authors and their works, and it is often a first point of research on essay questions. An example of an author-specific website that might be used for the essay question 'Discuss the role of nature in romantic poetry' is The Wordsworth Trust (www.wordsworth.org.uk). This site gives information on William Wordsworth himself, other writers he was associated with, the Romantic Movement and analysis of some of his major works, such as *The Prelude* or the poems he included in *Lyrical Ballads*.

Genre-specific websites give contextual information on a particular type of literature, including biographies and critical analyses of texts by authors, plus commentary on important cultural and historical themes within a movement. It is frequently important to be able to contextualize an author within a genre, and these websites can assist you with this task. So, for example, a website for the above essay question is 'The Romantic Movement in British Literature' (www.accd.edu/sac/english/bailey/engroman.htm), which has an extensive list of links under the categories 'Resources for Romanticism' and 'Specific Authors'.

Historical-period-based websites give contextual information focused on a specific period in history, which may include political, economic, social and cultural information. Knowing the historical

contexts for an author's work is intrinsic to understanding literature, since all writing is a product of the period from which it
emerges. An example of an unusual historical-period-based resource
for background information on the above essay title is the 'Eighteenth Century England' website (www.umich.edu/~ece/), which
contains projects by final-year literature students on different aspects
of eighteenth-century cultural history.

Bibliographic websites are important sources of information to
find other texts or websites on a given period, genre, work or
author. They often contain descriptions of each website or book so
that you can evaluate how important a particular resource may be
to you. These websites are particularly useful as a way into research,
to locate relevant resources that can be accessed at the beginning
of the research process for an essay. An example of a website like this
is Literary Resources on the Net (http://andromeda.rutgers.
edu/~jlynch/Lit/), which carries a bibliographic index of other
websites, focusing on most areas of English literature including
Romanticism, eighteenth century and Victorian literature, with
descriptive information on these websites.

'Books online' resources are now various and plentiful, covering
poetry, plays and novels, which are available in full-text versions on
the internet. They may be useful on many occasions, particularly if a
book you need has gone out of print or if there are no copies
available in the library, or if only a small number of poems, for
example, are needed for a particular lecture or seminar. They are
also searchable, which is useful if you are trying to track down a
phrase, word or image. A good example of a poetry online website
that could be used for the above essay question is English Verse
(www.englishverse.com), which contains over 750 poems from the
Middle English period to the twentieth century. For each author
there is some biographical and critical information.

Journals and newspapers online have been discussed in the journals section of this chapter. However it is worth noting that the *Times
Literary Supplement* has a website at http://tls.timesonline.co.uk,
which carries current articles and allows subscribers access to their
archive. As can be easily appreciated, these different types of website
all serve multiple purposes for English students. It is important to
use them regularly in order to make the best use of degree-level
study. Time spent investigating the resources available for your

research will be well spent online but there is now such a wealth of information available that you need to ensure you are focused in your inquiries.

How can I get access to the internet?

The internet can be accessed at a number of places both within your university and in the university's city or town. HEIs generally have a large number of computer rooms and terminals through which the internet can be accessed, both within their libraries and in specifically designed computer suites, although wireless internet connection (wifi) may be available in many zones if you have a suitably enabled laptop. Increasingly, there will also be broadband access within the student halls of residence.

For personal use of the web there are generally now internet cafes or shops within towns and cities. Also the internet can be accessed within the town or city's public library. There is generally no charge for this service, but usually a computer has to be booked in advance and the user has to be a member of the library. Wifi is also more and more common.

What search engines and websites should I use?

It is always preferable, and more reliable, to use academic search engines and websites when surfing the internet for university purposes because you can then be sure that a particular website is likely to be scholarly and of a good standard, usually written by experienced and qualified academics.

Examples of academic search engines, which would be useful for English students are Intute (www.intute.ac.uk/artsandhumanities), BUBLlink (http://bubl.ac.uk) and Google Scholar (http://scholar.google.com/ or go to www.google.co.uk and click on 'Scholar' on the main menu). When surfing, similar rules apply to searching for books or journals and these search engines include informative descriptions of the websites that appear on their result-lists so that you can evaluate their usefulness without having to follow each link. Another helpful resource is Pinakes: a subject launchpad (www.hw.ac.uk/libwww/irn/pinakes/pinakes.html) that has links to academic search engines for all subjects including those in the arts and humanities.

It is worth reiterating that care should be taken when searching the internet so that students can be sure they are using properly accredited and academic websites to ensure accuracy of information gained.

How can I make the best use of the internet?
The internet is a huge resource for students, but care must be taken in order to get the most from it; information on many sites is inaccurate, hence the need to use recognized search engines, and especially ones that are designed for students.

When searching, to achieve the best results always use an advanced search facility where possible. Also try to be precise, but not overly restrictive; it is advisable to use six to eight search terms when doing a search. Try to use phrases that seem natural. Use nouns as much as possible and try to avoid using verbs, adverbs, conjunctions and adjectives. Where possible it is advisable to make use of 'Boolean syntax', particularly the 'AND' function.[2]

There are online tutorials available, which will assist you greatly, listed in the further reading part of this section.

Libraries, LRCs and databases[3]

You should acquaint yourself early in your course with the appropriate sections of the library or Learning Resources Centre and its procedures and regulations. You will also find that library sessions for new students are a part of most English programmes. It is worth noting, however, that in addition to recommending books through the ordinary loan system, tutors may place in-demand texts on short loan or 'academic reserve'. Workshops may often also be held at various times during the academic year to acquaint you with the various electronic resources available.

The word *database* is a generic term for a collection of information held in a particular structured format. It can be applied to abstracts and indexes, and online journals and newspapers. Abstracts and indexes specialize in particular subject areas and pull together all essential information about journal articles. They can appear in various forms – online, DVD or print – and while indexes provide the bare facts (author, title, journal title and individual issue details), abstracts give the same information with the addition of a short summary about each article, which is more useful in helping you to decide which articles would be relevant to your research. Other useful texts to refer to are theses or dissertations, which present research and findings submitted for examination for a degree or professional qualification. A guide to theses published in the UK can be found online: www.theses.com/

Further help on research

BBC Key Skills: www.bbc.co.uk/keyskills/extra/module2/2.shtml

The Key Skills website gives basic advice on using books, journals and the internet, mainly in the form of observations and tips.

The Seven Steps of the Research Process: www.library.cornell.edu/olinuris/ref/research/skill1.htm

This website takes students through a seven-step guide to researching for assignments, with useful hints on and links for more information on each of the steps.

How to do Research in the Library: http://library.ucsc.edu/ref/howto

This website, from the University of California, Santa Cruz, allows students to sample all areas of research. It includes lists of relevant books and journal articles, as well as evaluating web resources.

Education World: Higher Education Community: Study Aids: www.education-world.com/higher_ed/study.shtml

This American website gives useful information on such topics as copyright and plagiarism. Also there are good links designed for undergraduates, listed under 'Undergraduate Study Aids'.

Researching on the internet
Bright Planet: www.brightplanet.com

This website contains a downloadable PDF resource on how to use the internet effectively. This is a detailed and informative tool for assistance with searching and using information on the internet.

Virtual Training Suite: www.vts.intute.ac.uk.

This website contains a virtual training suite for both further education and higher education English students. The training is of a practical nature, giving students the opportunity to practise their internet information skills.

INTUTE: Arts and Humanities: www.intute.ac.uk/ artsandhumanities

This website contains a search facility with over 18,000 web resources. As well as this, each entry contains a detailed description of the particular website's contents.

A Student's Guide to WWW Research: www.slu.edu/ departments/english/research/research.html

This website breaks down all aspects of internet research, in an easy to understand format.

Thinking Critically About World Wide Web Resources: www.library.ucla.edu/libraries/college/help/critical/

This website attempts a critical examination of the internet; how to look at websites and conduct research with critical questioning.

7 Writing

Reading is often the catalyst for writing but you also need to know when to stop. You will not be able to read everything on a subject, and assignments you are set will never be solely about reading; indeed they are likely to be primarily about writing or presenting. It is also not usually the best approach to do all your reading before beginning to write. Starting to fashion your thoughts in prose may well give you the best guide to what you need to read because it will probably illustrate where your knowledge and understanding are weak. This is particularly true of primary texts, which are the most important ones to read and re-read because an important principle in the writing and use of literary criticism is that, whatever the nature of the assignment you are required to do, you should never let the critic do the work for you. Use the views of others to support your own argument rather than as a substitute for it. Always remember that the marker wants to see evidence of *your* thinking about a subject in any assignment, rather than a demonstration of your skill in googling subjects or collecting books off the library shelf and transcribing quotations.

The skills, or disciplines, that the marker will want to see concern your writing practice. This covers your use of English (literacy skills), your argument (rhetorical skills), your essay form and structure (presentational skills), and your use of bibliographic and other conventions (scholarly skills).

Bibliographies, referencing and other conventions[1]

This section is more important than you might first think. Scholarly conventions enable tutors to read your essays effectively and to understand your use of others' work. At best, a poorly referenced assignment will frustrate your marker and reduce your grade; at worst it may have grave consequences if it is thought you are passing off others' work as your own. All departments will offer rules and also advice on how to use appropriate scholarly conventions in your work. The suggestions and recommendations below are indicative and are based on the guidelines in the *Modern Humanities Research Association Style Book*, which is a standard guide for humanities subjects, although there are others, especially the Harvard system, which is more commonly used in the sciences. The most important thing is consistency, so you should make sure that, whichever system you settle on, you use it carefully.

Quotations

- Employ quotation marks to indicate direct quotations and the definition of words (e.g. the word 'orange').
- In quoted passages follow the original spelling, punctuation, etc.
- Short quotations (approximately 40 words or two lines of verse) should be enclosed in single quotation marks ('. . . .') and run on with the main text.
- Double quotation marks (". . . .") are used for a quotation within a quotation.
- Longer quotations should start on a separate line, with no quotation marks and indented throughout.

Footnotes/endnotes and referencing

- Purpose: notes are used for documentation and citation of sources relevant to the text; notes should not duplicate information already made clear in the text.
- You can use footnotes, which appear at the bottom of each page, or endnotes, which are provided after the text.
- Notes should be numbered consecutively (1, 2, 3 . . .) throughout the text.
- Reference numbers are placed at the end of quotations (not following the author's name if this is given previously).
- If a quotation is not used, reference numbers are placed at the end of a sentence to interrupt the flow of the text as little as possible (alternatively you may insert one at a major break within a sentence if there will be more than one note).

- Reference numbers should be without punctuation and presented in superscript, appearing above the line of text, like this:[1]

Footnotes/endnotes and style

Notes should document information in the text in order to allow the reader to check the evidence on which an argument is based; the information given varies with the kind of text:

- Books: author (surname and initials), title underlined or in italics (and after the first full citation using a suitable and easily recognizable abbreviation for long titles), publication details in brackets (Place of Publication: Publisher, Year of Publication), page numbers (p. 15; pp. 14–16), for example:
  Author, *Title of Book* (London: Publisher, 1991) p. 15
- Articles: author, title of article in single quotation marks, name of journal underlined or in italics, volume number, year of publication, page reference, for example:
  Author, 'Title of Article', *Journal*, vol. 1, 1994, pp. 14–16
- Plays and poems: titles of plays and long poems should be underlined or in italics; titles of short poems and critical essays should be in single quotation marks.
- Titles of films are italicized (or underlined in hand-written script), and given with the director's name and the date of release, thus, for example:
  Citizen Kane (Welles, 1941)
- Internet sites: full details are required, including the date on which you accessed the article, for example:

  Author (if known), 'Title of internet article', Title of web page (if available), [accessed 1 January 2009], available from: http//www . . . (full website address).

Bibliography

- A bibliography should be presented on a separate sheet of paper after the text and notes detailing *all of the materials consulted* in the preparation of the essay (be particularly sure to include all works referred to in the text and notes).

- Bibliographical references are presented in alphabetical order by (first-named) author or editor/
- Bibliographical references should give the full title of the book (underlined or in italics) or article (in single quotation marks), name of journal (underlined or in italics) and full details of publication (place of publication: publisher, year).
- For style of presentation see the examples given above.

Finally, every HEI, at institutional, departmental or subject level, will have requirements for the presentation of your work in terms of the physical submission of the assignment. Most will also have an assignment cover sheet that must be submitted too, so that your details are known. A basic set of guidelines may look like the following.

General presentation

- Use white, A4 paper.
- With word-processed work, this should be double spaced with ample margins all around.
- Indent the first line of each paragraph.
- Word-processed work should be left-justified.
- Number pages consecutively in the top right-hand corner.
- Assignments should be carefully checked before submission for spelling, consistency, style, quotations against originals, etc.
- Do not staple the pages together; use a paper clip.
- Include student's name, module number and title, and name of module tutor on the first page.
- Give the full title (underlined) of the question being answered.
- ALWAYS retain a copy of your work.

Use of English

As discussed in the first chapter, one of the areas of most concern to lecturers in HE is students' writing ability. If you would like some guidance and help with your use of English, you will find there are now many websites that can assist. For example, some I would recommend are:

- The English Style Book: A Guide to the Writing of Scholarly English: www.litencyc.com/stylebook/stylebook.php

- Judy Vorfeld's Webgrammar site: www.webgrammar.com/
- The Purdue Online Writing Lab (OWL) (University of Purdue): http://owl.english.purdue.edu/
- Powerwrite: Grammar and Punctuation Help (Furman University): http://alpha.furman.edu/~moakes/Powerwrite/grammartoc.htm

Additionally, you will find many guides available in book form. Some I have found helpful to students are:

- *Cassell Guide to Common Errors in English*, by Harry Blamires
- *Cassell's Dictionary of English Grammar*, by James Aitchison
- *Grammar and Writing*, edited by Rebecca Stott and Peter Chapman
- *Write in Style*, by Richard Palmer
- *Grammar Guide*, by Gordon Jarvie

You will also find some older reference works at the end of the book in Further Reading, but the following are five important areas to consider if you want to think about your literacy skills:

1 Possessives and apostrophes

- The tree**'s** leaves = the leaves **of** the [single] tree.
- The trees**'** leaves = the leaves **of** the [plural] trees.
- [The tree**s** drop their leaves = a simple plural, not a possessive.]

- The car**'s** engine [= the engine **of** the car] is running well.
- The car**'s** running well = the car **is** running well [**not** a possessive].

All the above examples are correct, but the following one is not:

The car had it's engine serviced at the garage [incorrect: **its** should have no apostrophe in this case].

So, beware misusing 'its' and 'it's' especially:

- It**s** = **of** it or **belonging to** it [possessive]: it**s** coat is wet.
- It**'s** = it **is** [abbreviation of verb-phrase – as in the second 'car' example above]: it**'s** going to get it**s** coat wet. It's can also = it **has** [It's been raining].

2 'Subject-verb agreement'

Make sure **single subjects** have **single verb forms**. Ditto for **plurals**.

- The **sound** of fireworks **upsets** the dog.
- Firework**s** **upset** the dog.
- Before now, firework**s** **have** upset the dog.
- Before now, the **sound** of fireworks **has** upset the dog.

- Walking and reading **are** her favourite hobbies.
- Walking, not reading, **is** her favourite hobby.

- Each of us **is** going.
- None of us **is** going.
- All of us **are** going.

Beware collective nouns:

- A flock of sheep **was** in the road.
- The trade union **was** in turmoil.
- The trade unions **were** in turmoil.
- She **was** one of many writers who **were** there, and **was** pleased to be in their company.

3 'Fragments'

A 'fragment' is an incomplete sentence presented as a full sentence, in which something crucial – usually a **verb**, a **conjunction** ('and', 'but', 'since', etc.) or **punctuation** – is missing, for example:

- In the desert, I saw a wonderful sight. A long line of camels across the horizon. **[Wrong – no verb in second 'sentence'.]**

- Emma created quite a stir. <u>Wearing</u> a soldier's tunic. **[Wrong – no verb in second 'sentence'.]**

Citizens have a responsibility. <u>To vote</u> in every election. **[Wrong – no verb in second 'sentence'.]**

- Citizens have a responsibility *to vote* in every election. **[Right – one sentence.]**

- Citizens have a responsibility: to vote in every election. **[Right – colon links the second 'sentence' to the first.]**
- Citizens have a responsibility, *and should* vote in every election. **[Right – comma and conjunctive phrase inserted.]**
- Citizens have a responsibility, *which is* to vote in every election. **[Right – comma inserted and dependent clause created.]**

4 'Comma-splices'

A 'comma-splice' is the joining of two independent sentences or ideas with only a comma, for example:

- Bill hid his money under the floor, no one has ever found it. **[Wrong – two separate sentences 'spliced' with comma.]**
- Bill hid his money under the floor, *and* no one has ever found it. **[Right – comma and conjunction inserted.]**
- Bill hid his money under the floor; no one has ever found it. **[Right – semi-colon links two related clauses.]**
- Bill hid his money under the floor. *No* one has ever found it. **[Right – two complete sentences created.]**

5 Correct use of commas

It is difficult to give succinct but comprehensive and definitive advice on when and where to use **commas** properly: practice varies widely, with some writers using a great many and others very few. However, the commonest places in which commas should be used are:

- **In lists**, for example:
  There were apples, pears, bananas, peaches and grapes in the basket.
- **Where a sentence starts with an adverb or adverbial clause**, for example:
  Presently, the ship came into view.
  In all these respects, the book is a good one.
  At the beginning of the novel, Emma is a prig.

- **To join two or more related but separate parts of the same sentence**, for example:
  He was enjoying himself, but on the stroke of nine decided to leave.
  The novel is a good one, with many interesting characters, a good plot and a convincing setting.
- **To 'bracket off' a subsidiary clause in a sentence**, for example:
  The novel is a good one, although rather long, and contains many interesting characters.
  Peter, amongst many other people present, could not get a view of Emma.

A little test

Finally, if you want to test your English literacy skills as they are at present, try the little test below. There are 12 sections with five questions in each. If you score over 50 you should feel fairly confident about your abilities, although there may still be considerable room for improvement. If you score between 40 and 50 you should be working to improve your standard of English. If you score lower than 40, you need to work on your literacy skills urgently. The answers are given at the end of the book.

Yes or No?

---

1 Which of the following words are spelled correctly?

occassion
committee
neccessary
paralell
parliment

---

2 Which of the following words are spelled correctly?

cemetery
seperate
goverment
deceive
concious

3 Which of the following are sentences?

About a boy.

You thief.

Loves me like a rock.

You exist.

The sound of silence.

4 In which of the following sentences are all the commas correctly placed?

He is here, but, she is there.

They are going, now.

I am young, free and single.

No one knows, the trouble I have seen.

Entering the pub, I noticed her in the corner.

5 Which of these sentences make sense?

Coming round the mountain, the pub appeared in the distance.

Going to Mars, the astronauts would need copious supplies.

Looking out of the window, the car was at the end of the street.

Thinking quickly, I gave the necessary reply.

Though they were passed their sell-by date, the men ate the eggs.

6 Which of these sentences have an excess word?

This ever-changing world in which we live in is too fast for me.

The last thing of which I thought of was my own safety.

I want to buy a house on the street you live on.

The school to which she went to was far away.

Of the five remaining, two were highly thought of by the selection panel.

7 In which of these sentences is the semi-colon correctly used?

I am old; you are young.

There are three people in the room; Sue, John and Mary.

He is late; you should go.

The cat is by the door and; the dog is by the fire.

It is time; to go.

8 Which of the following could be considered grammatically correct?

It is hot, the sun is shining.

It is hot: the sun is shining.

It is hot. The sun is shining.

It is hot; the sun is shining.

It is hot and the sun is shining.

---

9   Which of these sentences are grammatically correct?

We would of gone tomorrow.

They gave the tickets to you and I.

He is over their.

It is I.

Nobody effects me.

---

10   Which of these sentences imply that judges should not take sides?

Judges should be disinterested.

Judges should be impartial.

Judges should be uninterested.

Judges should be partial.

Judges should be unbiased.

---

11   In which of these sentences are the apostrophes used correctly?

It's a dog's life.

That's the dog's bone.

It's a girl.

Every dog has it's day.

It's raining men.

---

12   In which of these phrases are the apostrophes used correctly?

It's a man's bag!

The womens' movement.

Boys' don't cry.

The girls' have left.

The working-men's club.

8 Note-taking, lectures and revision

Lecturer A: 'I thought you said you'd taught the students that.'
Lecturer B: 'Yes, but I didn't say they'd learned it.'

Note-taking

One-hour lectures are perhaps the strangest experience for new students in higher education. There may be little in your previous studies to prepare you for this learning experience. Still more unnerving for many freshers is the fact that note-taking skills of the kind required by lectures are unlikely to have been covered in your education before going to university.

At school, for example, you may have been used to taking copious notes; but this is not the best way to approach lectures, as tutors will not be looking for you to regurgitate their material in your essays – and you would need to have excellent shorthand skills to keep up anyway! Nonetheless, this is a common approach that new students take to lectures. Remarking on this, Keverne Smith advises that 'In reality, an effective response to a lecture requires selective note-taking and an ability to recognize the overall shape of the lecture and to register the hierarchy of ideas being presented; it requires an overview.'[1]

Many students unhappily expect lecturers to dictate notes but today this will be rare (unless there is a key quotation, for example) even though dictation was part of the original purpose of lectures in the Middle Ages before print technologies. Some lecturers nowadays will use PowerPoint or handouts to provide an overview of the lecture, its key points, or the quotations used. Although lectures are a good way of putting over a wealth of ideas to large numbers of students, especially as seminar preparation, Smith found that only 34 per cent of students felt well prepared for note-taking in lectures and he concluded that the lecture 'is not the main or the most conducive aspect of the learning experience'.

Consequently, you will find that some courses will hardly use lectures at all or will use shorter lectures, especially in the first year. Several departments have now introduced note-taking guidance into early lectures and 'icebreaking' exercises. In terms of practical advice, you would be best advised in lectures to: sit near the front to ensure you can hear well; think about what is being said and why before you write anything down; engage with the argument rather than try to note down or remember what is said verbatim; go along as well prepared as possible because prior reading will be beneficial; write up or reorganize your notes afterwards; remember the lecturer is speaking from a point of view and so is not simply giving you facts or telling you what to think. Lectures are there to help you gain an overview of the topic in hand, and so your primary role is to listen and reflect, not to write.

Similarly, the primary role of reading is to spur your thought and so note-taking outside of lectures is best undertaken with this in mind. Note-taking should always have a purpose, and this may affect your choice of technique: note-cards, underlining, highlighting, marginalia, A4 notes, *aide memoirs* or typing at a computer. In general, it is good advice to see note-taking and reading as simultaneous activities; but, if this disturbs instead of focuses your thoughts, you may want to make notes later, for example using 'mind maps' to show the connections between parts of your reading.

Many universities will also have workshop sessions on writing, speaking, listening and thinking skills. Additionally, you may find lecturers introduce elements of 'dialogue' into their sessions with you, by putting forward different interpretations of texts, for example, to encourage debate. This is to stress that the purpose of university-level study is to stimulate the process of learning, which in the humanities is best understood as sharpening your understanding and your analytical skills. The acquisition of knowledge is very important but often not as important as the uses to which you put it. What you are therefore attempting to identify when note-taking are main points, themes, new ideas and questions, connections with your previous learning, potentially helpful references, and material for discussion or debate.

In summary, you will probably want to take some notes during lectures; many of the citations or references given during lecture sessions are invaluable and should be followed up independently. You should not, however, attempt to record the lecture at the expense of listening and, more particularly, at the expense of thinking. This is not to make English studies a confrontational affair; it is rather to stress that it should be an interactive and, indeed, creative process of learning in which you aim to survey, question, read, recall and review.[2]

New technologies

Word-processing packages provide excellent means of organizing, spell checking and revising your work. They also allow you to determine the word-count, which is helpful throughout the process of writing. Essays should go through several drafts, and you should ensure you proofread your work at the end: the worst impression to give to the marker is that you couldn't be bothered to check your work before submitting it.

There have also been a number of recent initiatives using electronic resources as an additional teaching and learning method. In some cases, the use of Blackboard or WebCT (products that enable universities to host classes on the world wide web) as a source of information, interaction and discussion may be either optional or a requirement on a module. These are usually available as an additional resource to enrich knowledge and open up discussion, as are printed resource-packs, audio-visual materials, corpora and a range of electronic media, especially on courses that have developed distance-learning resources. In addition to PowerPoint, you may also find lecturers use podcasts, really simply syndication (RSS) streaming, weblogs or other adjuncts to their teaching, but always remember that the primary purpose of education is not teaching, but learning.

As noted earlier in Chapter 6, your decision how to use the internet is one of the most important ones. Your bibliography must show where your ideas have come from and lecturers will not be impressed with a list of references to sites you have found via Google, for example. Selective web use for information checking and for tracking down helpful scholarly work is good practice, but remember that the web is an uncontrolled repository for the most part and the majority of material has not been through the checks and review processes that paper-published work usually has. Also, be sure what your motives are for using the web rather than for reading – webwork tends to be quick and easy but that is rarely what the tutor marking your essay will be wanting from you. The best use of library computers is often to track down paper-based reading that your lecturers will have requested the learning centre or library to stock for you.

Revision strategies

Revise selectively, but in an organized and directed way. First and foremost be clear on the rubric and format for the exam, and especially on two points: do you know how many and what kind of questions you will be asked to answer; do you know on what texts or topics the questions might be asked? You may want to select your revision topics and texts on the basis of the number of different question-areas they would allow you to tackle, or choose to revise the ones you know best and then see what your options would be. In any case, you should try to decide before the examination the texts you would like to use to answer a question on possible subjects (this does not mean you cannot change your mind in the exam). You might also want to think about specific points you would like to make, and particular critics/theorists you would want to discuss. All of this can be done in advance, with the aim of allowing you to use your understanding imaginatively in the exam.

Suggested areas to revise for most literature exams are:

(a) **Langage usage** (imagery, style, tone, character construction, syntax, allusions, descriptions, etc.).

(b) **Identity** (of all kinds, and especially in terms of gender, sexuality, ethnicity, class, childhood, nationality and so on; e.g. for texts concerned with the post–colonial, where the writer/narrator/character is from, their colonial history, their relation to colonial/post-colonial events, their allegiances, their sense of hybridity or mimicry, the constructions of colonial discourse [e.g. stereotypes], parody, polemic, and the assertions of national/post–colonial independence, the relation between colonized and colonizer).

(c) **Narrative form** (imitative, historical, fantastical, first/third person, long/short narrative, order of events, divisions between book's sections, etc.).

(d) **Historical situation**: changes in politics, art, technology and science, etc.

(e) **Differences/specificities of key cultural aspects** such as 'race', gender, and nation in terms of author, narrator and characters.

(f) Concern with psychology and use of unusual or multiple **perspectives** (in modernist work, for example, cubist perspectives, multiple or repeated narration, collage, doppelgangers, underground or shell-shocked characters, etc.).

(g) Aspects to poetic analysis. It may be useful to have a mnemonic that will prompt you to cover key elements, for example:

- **C**apitalizations
- **R**hyme scheme
- **A**llusion and alliteration
- **F**irst line
- **T**heme
- **V**ersification
- **I**magery
- **P**ersonification
- **E**njambement/line ends
- **R**hythm
- **S**entence construction.

NB. Many of these overlap and the list is by no means exhaustive.

Practical advice for revision is to: start early; plan your time; work with others; use mnemonics or other memory aids; and consult previous exam papers. Above all, the best way to prepare is to try sample questions. If you attempt a previous paper's question under exam conditions you will not only find out how you perform, you will learn more: as an occasional practice-technique, the intense experience of doing a mock-exam question for yourself will probably be a better use of an hour than reading. Exams are not memory tests; they are opportunities to deploy the understanding you have of a topic or text in a creative, analytical and engaging way.

Exams

Exams in English vary and you may find you are asked, for example, to write three essays in three hours, to offer a reading of a poem or extract (gobbet), to define some terms, or to write several small essays. For all of these you can plan and practise your answers by setting yourself exercises in advance of the examination.

Several things affect your performance in exams. Of these, arguably the most important are your:[3]

1   Knowledge
2   History of exam success
3   Exam preparation
4   Exam practice
5   Writing skills
6   Use of time
7   Approach.

In the exam hall, take some time to read through the entire examination paper once, to decide which are the best questions to answer and to get a sense of how the examiners are covering the syllabus through the questions. This is also the time to think about which texts you will be using in your answers.

A next step is to draw up a plan for your answers, ensuring that you do not duplicate your material and that you have a structure for your response to each question. You should then have the confidence to tackle the questions calmly and methodically.

(a) For an extract analysis: go through it once to appraise its literary aspects (style, tone, metaphors, narrative perspective, colloquialisms, repetitions, omissions, dialogue, intertextualities, characters, suspense, vocabulary, etc.); go through it again to pick up on themes relevant to the (author and the) longer work itself – you may also want to refer to the passage's position in the overall narrative, but do not use this as an excuse to 'tell the story'; go through it once more looking for events or 'keywords' you can discuss in terms of historical themes.

(b) For an essay: avoid discussing texts too literally – do not summarize the plot of a novel and do not paraphrase. Pick out the keywords in the essay question and be sure to discuss them. If you have read relevant critical or theoretical works, cite them or their authors. If the question has a quotation, think about it, but answer the question not the quotation.

Finally, you should leave time at the end of the session to read through your answers and make any corrections. This allows you the opportunity to tidy up any infelicities of expression or sentence construction as well as put right errors.

PART THREE:
Assessment: making the grade

Having started to look at approaches towards assessment in the last part, including the particular test of the exam, I will be looking in this section at other forms of assessment and the ways you can handle them. The English Benchmarking Statement stipulates that 'programmes in English should articulate principles of coherent and progressive development across the curricular provision and the learning experience of students'. The assessment tasks used to measure the achievement of learning outcomes by students thus aim to test ideas and subject knowledge as well as skills of problem solving, research, comprehension and analysis.

The primary tool used in non-examination assessment in English is the essay, to which the Benchmark Statement draws specific attention, because it enables you to engage in sustained written debate with ideas and display the understanding and knowledge you have acquired in a structured way. The essay, or article, is also the primary means by which research in English is disseminated in journals and books. However, you may also be assessed by seminar presentation, performance or even appearance, by group work, seen class-test, unseen exam, close reading exercise, research task or study-skills assessments, or by a number of other less common means such as writing a book review or making an anthology.

From the table, it can be deduced that results for English students compare favourably with those achieved by undergraduates on related subjects. The overwhelming majority of students, approximately 90 per cent, emerge with a second-class degree. This state of affairs, once realized, means that many students see their performance almost exclusively in terms of a 2(i) or a 2(ii) degree result: the former being the desired grade to indicate above average performance. This was not the case 20 years ago, for example when a 2(ii) was at least as common as, if not more common than, a 2(i), and was considered the most expected degree result.

Degree classes – 2000 HESA data. Students obtaining a classified degree from their first degree course						
Class of degree	English		History, archaeology & classics		Languages, linguistics & area studies	
First class	448	9%	701	9%	1224	9%
Upper second	2969	60%	4550	61%	7527	59%
Lower second	1439	29%	2105	28%	3876	30%
Third	108	2%	159	2%	330	2%
Total	**4964**		**7515**		**12 957**	

(Source: English Subject Centre/HESA
www.english.heacademy.ac.uk/explore/publications/newsletters/
newsissue5/hestats.htm)

All universities, and English departments within them, will have marking criteria. These indicate the difference between a 'pass' and 'fail' grade, but they also indicate the different expectations of work that falls into the grade classifications, as well as some areas within them; for example, within 'first class' it is possible to talk of a 'good first', which is useful to funding bodies (such as the Arts and Humanities Research Council (AHRC)) when deciding between students who apply for grants to do postgraduate work.

Pass marks may vary but it is common for this to be set at 40, which is the threshold for a third-class degree if a student is graduating with honours (*cum laude*). Next is the 2(ii) classification spanning from 50–59, 2(i) from 60–69, and first from 70–100. An example of broad criteria used in the classification of assessment marks is given below as a basic guideline. Additionally, specific criteria for each piece of assessment will most likely be provided on course materials distributed at the beginning of each module or unit, and these will be linked to the 'learning outcomes' set.

Mark	Descriptor
80–100 or 'A' grade outstanding	Everything in the 'excellent' category but with evidence of an additional capacity for original thought and independent judgement, and the ability to relate the topic/question to a wider context/framework.
70–79 or 'A' grade excellent	Comprehensive grasp of the question and all major issues involved. Wide range of sources used. Clear structure. Detailed critical and theoretical analysis. Excellent organization and argument. Adept use of language, spelling and grammar. Capacity to look at issues from several standpoints and to synthesize viewpoints as well as draw a sound conclusion. Wide bibliography and careful footnoting.
60–69 or 'B' grade	Well-focused on the question. Shows a sound grasp of the key issues of debate involved in the topic. Good use of both primary and secondary source material. Sound organization and a well-structured argument. Capacity to engage with the material and issues arising from it. Ability to engage with critical and theoretical perspectives.
50–59 or 'C' grade	Demonstrates a grasp of the question and engages with the key issues. Shows evidence of reading and an ability to assimilate recommended texts. Material shows evidence of shape and coherence. Assignment either lacks depth of analysis or is overly dependent on description or secondary material.
40–49 or 'D' grade	Shows superficial understanding of the question. Not focused on key issues. Material may be partly relevant, but is not well-organized or presented. Lack of clear conclusion. Little evidence of general reading.

(Continued)

| 30–39 or 'F' grade | Failure to engage with the question. Inadequate use of sources. No evidence of general reading. Lack of content. Misunderstanding of the basic issues. |
| 0–29 or 'F' grade | Very little material relevant to the question. |

While these guidelines indicate the general criteria required for each grade, it is also important to understand that expectations will change throughout your degree according to the notion that both the subject-specific and transferable skills you acquire at each level will be built upon in the next. Poor use of English, spelling, punctuation and grammar will nearly always reduce your mark but the reduction will not usually be quantified.

In general, assessment over the levels will require a growing amount of autonomy and a development from a broad to a specialized knowledge base. Thus, a higher proportion of sophistication in your argument, a more developed sense of judgement, and an increasingly independent approach to learning will be expected at each level. For example, at level 1 it may not be a requirement that you regularly consult secondary source material, although many lecturers and tutors will recommend books and articles that could enhance your understanding. By level 2, however, it is likely to be an expectation that you regularly consult secondary material, including journals, and that you refer to this reading in your written and seminar work. Finally, at level 3, it is normal to expect you to exercise a critical facility in selecting and commenting on the material you find in your independent research.

9 Seminars/presentations

Although teaching practice varies, perhaps the most common approach to learning in contact time on HE English courses combines seminars and lectures. Of the two formats, a majority of university teachers favour the more flexible and open forum that a seminar situation provides. Many modules that do have lectures stage them at regular intervals or at specific points in the programme rather than have them every week. When combined, seminars commonly follow a lecture, with the aim of discussing ideas and approaches that have been suggested by the lecturer.

Seminar

A 'seminar' is the name given to discussion classes of, usually, between about five and 25 students. Smaller sessions would more likely be 'tutorials'. The seminar is, for most students, the hub of the contact-time learning experience. You must therefore ensure that you have done the required reading and are both well prepared and willing to participate actively in the seminar. Seminars are designed to enable fuller and more active student participation than a lecture situation affords. The word seminar derives from the Latin *seminarium* meaning 'seed-bed' and it might be useful to think of the seminar as an opportunity for the dissemination and exchange of ideas. Seminars should promote the exploration as well as the acquisition of knowledge. Keverne Smith found that 54 per cent of students felt well prepared for contributing to seminar discussion, and 32 per cent adequately prepared. This is a better response than for lectures, and while 33 per cent thought all teaching methods were equally valuable, 50 per cent thought they learned more from seminar discussion than from any other method.[1]

Seminars can operate in many different ways. Sometimes the

whole seminar group will be involved in a general discussion, or the group may be given a specific focus, textual exercise or topic. Small group-work is also common. Sometimes a seminar will be 'student-led' and this often involves individual presentations. These presentations will reflect an individual's research but should also invite queries from, and ask questions of, the rest of the seminar group. The role of the tutor in seminars can be very flexible. As seminars are not 'lessons' as such, the tutor is there not only to impart information or provide answers but also to guide the discussion. On some modules, seminar work additionally forms part of the assessment component, but in all cases your fullest participation is seen as necessary for a successful and generally satisfying learning experience.

Studying one or two subjects requires a high degree of specialization at university, which means that English students are likely to have a concentrated skills set too. Pre-university work will focus on both note-taking and group discussion, which is helpful for seminar work. Often the tutor will recommend that you work on a particular question or topic or text in small numbers of four to six students. This provides a good chance to learn from each other and to talk through the issues without feeling that the whole class is involved, which can be intimidating. Working in subsets is also a step towards independent learning, which your tutor will be keen to encourage, and this is an element that is likely to increase over the course of the degree. Unlike most lectures, seminars rely on participation and are opportunities for active learning, as opposed to the more passive environment of the lecture room. The seminar leader will sometimes ask you to discuss ideas in your sub-group and then report back to the whole (plenary) group. The tutor is likely to query some of your feedback or seek clarification in order to tease out the key salient points for all the students in the seminar as well as add their own specialist viewpoint. Contributions will always be valued but a good seminar tutor will aim to ensure that all students participate and that a few voices do not dominate.

As Smith notes, the seminar has been more favoured on English courses than the lecture in recent years as it is considered 'that knowledge is more a matter of perception and analysis of conflicting interpretations than had been thought for much of the twentieth century'. Opinions, ideas, perspectives, debate, argument and analytical depth are often more important than facts, but some students will still unfortunately say they find the latter more important for their note-taking. According to studies, most students feel reasonably well prepared for seminars and believe they take away more than they do from other teaching methods. Within this, the seminar debate or presentation is an extremely useful method of learning for those who speak and for those who listen and respond. Two types of presentation are common.

The first is in groups, when a subset of the overall seminar group may be asked to make a short presentation on an author or an aspect of a text or context. The particular form of the presentation will vary according to the tutor who sets it and the students who plan it, but the following are possible formats:

- Individual students in the group are assigned to speak on different aspects of the same topic.
- A series of overheads are individually prepared by members of the group but introduced by a 'compère'.
- A jointly prepared 'diagram' of the topic might be explained jointly.
- A rehearsed reading of material jointly researched by all the group members.

The most important factor in group work is to ensure that everyone takes an equal share and that, while tasks will be different, each member of the group has a sense of shared ownership. The activity of a group presentation is one of the best for gaining experience helpful to teamwork, interaction and cooperation in the workplace. However, most of the advice for a group presentation is the same as for an individual one, so this will be discussed next as the second type of common presentation format regularly included in seminars. [2]

How to give a presentation

Most students will be asked to give a presentation at some point in their studies, and this is excellent practice for future working life. The fundamental key to presentations is the familiar phrase: 'prior preparation prevents poor performance'. The crucial term here is of course 'preparation' and this can be separated into three parts: people, planning and practice.

The 3 Ps: people, planning, practice

People

Although you will be thinking a great deal during your preparation about your own likely experience of the presentation, the most important people in the room are going to be your audience.

So, to begin your preparation, ask yourself two questions:

- Who is my audience and what is their current knowledge or understanding?
- What do I want my audience to LEARN or DO as a result of my presentation?

These questions should help to focus your approach to the pitch (or level), structure (or organization) and material (or content) of your presentation.

How can I keep the audience interested?

This is not just a matter of content, but also of style. What aids are you using to help your audience understand your argument? Are you thinking about whether you are engaging and animated? Are you going to practise modulating your voice to emphasize and accentuate different points and words?

People respond best to others, and presentations in particular, if they are both interested in the topic and involved in the speaker's academic investment in it. Try to put yourself in their place and imagine the queries they might have. Such questions are perhaps those you should seek to answer in the course of your presentation.

Also, aim wherever possible to keep the presentation simple while remembering that simple is not the same as simplistic. Simple means straightforward and to the point – if your presentation is convoluted or too detailed your audience will lose interest. You also do not have to explain everything; just your key points and the thrust of your argument.

Planning

Your presentation will have a structure whether you realize it or not. If you do not pay attention to how your talk is organized, however, you will confuse your audience, put things in the wrong order, and have no clear sense of time, direction or purpose. Structure is important – your presentation should have a beginning, a middle and an end. You may want to explain this to your audience too, so they know where you are in your argument. The key elements of an essay in which you explain what you are doing, do it, and then explain what you have done, are also good ingredients for a presentation.

Therefore, your beginning should aim to tell your audience in a succinct and engaging way what you are going to proceed to explore with them or explain to them later. Be positive throughout and try to engage the people in the audience's attention – they will only be interested in your topic if you are, so be sure to take them with you in your enthusiasm. Speak directly and clearly, make eye contact, and let them know you are interested in their attention and their reactions. The guidelines here are similar to those for an interview situation.

The middle section of your presentation will be the longest and may have several parts. Structure this with a logical sequence that develops from one area or topic to another – probably by using verbal queues or visual links to guide the audience. The whiteboard, PowerPoint and overhead transparencies can also be of considerable assistance here and may help you to link each bit of the presentation in a less formal way than you would in an essay.

The end of your presentation should include a brief summary or reiteration of the key points. You could use handouts or a bullet-point style here, but you may also want to summarize your overall analysis with an apposite quotation or with a well-chosen sentence that encapsulates the nub of your argument. Finally, thank your audience.

Practice

Practice will help with timing, confidence, your expression and your sense of speaking to a 'room'. You should also practise in the seminar room beforehand if possible, but at the very least you

should try out any equipment before you use it in the actual presentation. If you are able, practise in front of someone else and get some
feedback on your performance: speed, clarity, structure and level of
engagement are all useful subjects to get some comments on.

The following are a few hints and tips for you to consider when
making the presentation:

- Talk at a medium pace and breathe slowly.
- Speak up and project your voice appropriately, but do not
  shout – be conscious of the volume you are speaking at.
- Pace, tone and inflection are important. Speaking in a mono-
  tone voice is very tedious for the audience – be enthusiastic
  and engaged but not pedantic or hectoring.
- Beware using jargon, acronyms or colloquialisms. Not everyone speaks the same (technical) language – use full phrases and
  avoid slang terms.
- Always stand if you can. It may seem more daunting, but it
  gives you confidence and helps with voice projection.
- Be conscious of your gestures – look at news presenters if you
  want to get an idea of how much and how little to use your
  hands.
- If you are nervous, holding something in your hand can calm
  you but be careful not to shake it or play with it. Do not wave
  your hands about but do not keep them firmly stuffed in your
  pockets either.

Using audio visual equipment
Do:

- Use landscape rather than portrait.
- Remember the 6, 7, 8 rule – no more than six lines to an
  overhead or slide, use letters no less than 7mm high, and
  employ no more than eight screens or acetates for a 10 minute
  presentation.
- Check your spelling, punctuation and grammar.
- Focus the projector and then check everyone can see.
- Use a consistent format to the slides.
- Stop talking when you change transparencies and avoid
  simply reading them out.

- Provide your audience with a handout copy.
- Use pictures and diagrams to illustrate your points but not to make them.

Do not:

- Talk too fast.
- Umm and aah, fidget or fiddle.
- Block the people in the audience's view or turn your back to them.
- Put too many points onto a slide/acetate.
- Write up to the edge (leave a margin instead).
- Point at the screen unless you have a pointing device.
- Leave the projector light on between transparencies.
- Use too many colours.

What is the marker looking for?

With a presentation, the markers will be looking for understanding of the topic as well as for strengths in relevant skills: fluency, articulacy, coherence, pace, delivery, audibility and the ability to engage the audience. Additional resources may be of benefit to your presentation but do not use them indiscriminately or gratuitously. Content is usually more important than form in most presentations, so remember that the markers will be looking at subject-specific factors in addition to your skills at presenting material. For example, one university assessment pro forma for a group presentation states:

The presentations will be assessed according to the following criteria:

- The cogency of the argument presented.
- Effective use of the time available (maximum 15 minutes).
- Evidence of collaboration and team-work in planning and presentation.
- Capacity to generate further discussion.

The assessment criteria for your presentation will not be the same as this, but you do need to focus on the elements the markers will be looking for, so ensure that you have the relevant information to hand when you are preparing it. The remaining advice to offer for presentations has to focus on attitude. If you can, try to relax, be confident and enjoy it; the worst part of presenting for many people is the anticipation, rarely the performance.

10 Close textual analysis

The skilful and creative analysis of a text, whether a poem, a prose extract or a piece of recorded speech, lies near to the heart of English studies. Such analysis often lies behind the phrase 'reading the text' or 'close reading', and in many ways detailed analytical reading is the aspect of English studies that is most distinctive. There are few disciplines in which you will be regularly asked to consider the language of a piece of writing in such detail. It is also one of the key points at which English literature, English language and creative writing meet. All these related disciplines are interested in the use of words and their combination. There will be a chapter considering studying language and practising writing later in this book, but here I will consider textual analysis as it applies to reading literature.

The first thing that might be considered is the title, if the piece has one. Its relation to the rest of the text is important (does the title refer to a person, a place, a symbol or a well-known phrase, for example). An important consideration here is whether the title is primarily referential or metaphoric (compare, for example, *David Copperfield* or *Northanger Abbey*, which respectively name a person and a house, with *The Heart of the Matter* or *The Turn of the Screw*). Considering whether the title is primarily denotative (as in descriptive) or connotative (that is, suggestive and allusive) is useful but it is also important to consider the range of meanings that a title could have because there may be more than one, as with *Enduring Love*, for example. A further aspect that can be considered before analysing a poem or extract in detail is the layout of the text: how it looks on the page. This is in terms of paragraph length, typography, ellipses, dashes and so on, as well as such aspects as the use of short or long lines/sentences, speech marks, sub-divisions or headings.

Within the text under analysis, quotations and allusions are important features that you should always think about. These may be flagged up, as often happens under the title for example, or may be submerged – without any acknowledgment. The crucial point is that you should be alive to 'borrowed' or familiar phrases and to words which seem to be 'freighted' with extra significance, because allusions can be made to almost anything: contemporary events, popular culture, religion, politics, folk tales, limericks, poems, (auto)-biography or scientific theories. Usually, these are connections known to the author, but any phrase or piece of text can be add-itionally considered in terms of its status as 'discourse' – its use of expressions and terms familiar from non–literary contexts (e.g. religious, historical, popular cultural or political). All of these can be remarked upon because they indicate facets of the text, in terms of class, gender, education, ethnicity, beliefs, prejudices and so on.

As with the title, there is only one first line or sentence and it serves as a prelude to the rest of the text. Even in an extract, the opening sentence has a unique position, and this is partly why there are many famous opening lines or sentences but few second or third ones. You should therefore consider the effect that the initial line or sentence has. Does it orient you by giving information? Does it throw you into the narrative as though you had entered a story in the middle? Is it in speech marks? Is it authoritative or hesitant, succinct or rambling? How is it arranged in terms of word order?

Imagery is a crucial part of any text's effects, and comes in many guises and places. Significant imagery may be present in the title, or apparent in repeated references, or created through descriptions, metaphors or similes. Every use of language that is not (meant to be) literal is a form of imagery and can be profitably analysed (very few uses of language are in fact not figurative). For example, you might consider whether the image has a relevance to the general subject matter of the text, whether it is an image from nature or culture, or even whether much of the imagery in a text is consist-ently similar (to create a particular effect on the reader, whether it be romantic, eerie or comical, for example). The most important types of figures of speech to look out for are metaphors, metonyms, personification, similes and synecdoche.

Another distinctive aspect to any piece of writing is its style. Here you should consider the vocabulary and grammar of the extract, the tone, the ratio of narration to dialogue, the use of (especially unusual) punctuation, the employment of dialect, contractions, adjectives or adverbs, passive sentences, specialized terms and colloquialisms – again, in this light you should also think about qualities that have been mentioned before such as imagery, figurative language and repetitions. Further aspects to the language that might be considered, especially in an analysis of poetry, are: emphasis (exclamation marks, capitalized words, italicization), use of alliteration (consonant repetitions, as in 'seven sins') or assonance (vowel repetitions, as in 'bee-keeper'), and rhythm (important when discussing poetry as well as the fiction of modernist writers such as James Joyce, Virginia Woolf, or E.M. Forster). One more thing to add to this list is structure, which can depend upon rhythm. Structure does not just mean whether or not the piece seems organized, but whether it is discernibly patterned or designed.

There are four other aspects to close reading that should be considered here. They require a little more explication but are useful components of an analytical vocabulary and a specialist terminology: spatial reading, intertextuality, irony and prolepsis. The concept of 'spatial reading' was derived from the idea that modern-(ist) art is pervaded by a philosophical formalism that amounts to a 'style' (as opposed to nineteenth-century 'stylization') that requires the reader to be more active and highly self-conscious. This is mainly because of the text's complex construction, which works against drawing conclusions from any part of it before the finish is reached. A parallel example is with land surveying, which is nigh impossible from flat ground and needs to take place at an elevated level. The idea of spatial reading largely derives from the cubist art movement, which argues that a three-dimensional object or event ought to be analysed from all angles and not just one, as in traditional painting. Spatial reading is particularly important when looking at modernist fictional texts that deploy terms repeatedly across their narratives, such as *Heart of Darkness*, where a complex, rhythmical usage of words such as 'light' and 'dark' militates against any straightforward understanding of their meanings, which are necessarily always partial and provisional.

A second key consideration is that when discussing any piece of literature, readers should think about influences, allusions and references to other texts. A different way of approaching this is in terms of 'intertextuality', which, as a concept, acknowledges that a text is not simply the work of an author in isolation. Any piece of writing deploys language drawn from many textual systems (usages from the law, aesthetics, mythology and so on) in one 'weave' by threading together strands of social discourse. A text is never original in the sense that the words it employs, if not the expressions, are to be found elsewhere (in intertexts), even though the text is original in the sense that it is a unique arrangement of those words.

Third, 'irony', which is pervasive in poetry and prose, occurs whenever appearance and reality differ. This is even though, in a limited verbal sense, 'irony' refers to a figure of speech in which one meaning of a word or expression clashes with an alternative meaning. In most literary criticism, intentional irony has generally been admired as a quality of textual complexity, but it is also common now to consider ironies in the text irrespective of authorial intention, precisely because the flexibility and plurality of meaning in relation to language allows multiple interpretations of almost any utterance. So, on the one hand, all language is ambiguous and has a plurality of meaning, and, on the other hand, all language is narrated. Who is speaking is always a key question, and it may have more than one answer. The opening sentence to Jane Austen's *Pride and Prejudice* is spoken directly by the narrator. For many readers, this narrator is synonymous with Austen herself. Alternatively, it soon becomes clear that the view expressed in the opening sentence is not that of the narrator, let alone the author, but of Mrs Bennet. In other words, a case can be made for thinking that the opening words of the novel are those of a character, of the author (or an 'implied' author), or simply of the narrator. The key point is that when readers identify a piece of writing as 'ironic', they are asserting that it does not mean what it appears to at face value, and so are opening up a gap between what the text says and what it means: a reading practice that, because of the ability of language to mean so many things, including the opposite of what we initially take it to mean, can be expanded to all kinds of interpretations that read between the lines of texts. For many critics, it is precisely this richness of narration and speech in literature that makes it such a fertile and 'open' genre. For example, the voice of any one character in a novel will be a meeting point for all sorts of overt and covert discourses, or viewpoints, which will themselves be put into competition with other discourses and voices, creating an enormously complex tapestry of language, in which stresses and emphases can be placed not only on what the text says but on what it does not say.

Fourth, 'prolepsis' is the anticipation of an utterance or an event that has yet to occur or be narrated. Strictly speaking, prolepsis requires that a future event be treated as though it is currently happening (e.g. 'I am gone'), but critics use it more loosely to refer to allusions to, and foreshadowings of, later incidents in the narrative. For example, Robinson Crusoe speaks on the opening page of his narrative of 'the life of misery that was to befal me', explicitly placing current events and descriptions in the light of what has not yet been narrated. Prolepsis is a figure of speech that can be used either to anticipate some future incident's connection with that which is currently being narrated, or simply to create suspense, but it can also work at the level of language, where words and phrases themselves can be linked to future ones, or phrases can be built up before it is known to what they refer (e.g. see the opening sentence of *Paradise Lost* where the main verb – 'sing' – is repeatedly delayed). Additionally, telling the story with hindsight, as with *Jane Eyre* (Charlotte Brontë), *Tintern Abbey* (Wordsworth) or *Great Expectations* (Dickens), is a common method through which narrators introduce a sense of a double-perspective, speaking, to different degrees, as both older and younger self. A further technique to create suspense by introducing two timeframes is to begin the story at its end, as many films do and a novel such as Malcolm Lowry's *Under the Volcano* does.

The question should also be raised of the omnipresence of not narrators but narrative. To begin with, it is obvious that narrative is not exclusive to fiction. Films, television programmes, plays, songs and poetry all contain narrative: they all tell stories, using images and/or words. The more difficult question to ask is: what uses of language, or of visual imagery, do not contain narrative? Does a bank statement have a narrative? Does the description of a scientific experiment have one? Do the workings of a mathematical calculation?

Although we would want to make distinctions between kinds of narrative, we would probably give an affirmative answer to each of these questions. All of these examples are concerned with narrative in that they are concerned with causation. They all tell stories by arranging events in an order, with one event succeeded by another that in some sense follows on from it. This brings us to one important element of narrative: time. Stories tell us about change over time, and so does a bank statement: your bank balance has gone down because you wrote a cheque, took some money out, or had to pay bank charges and so on.

More difficult examples would be photographs, shopping lists or telephone directories. These are more problematic because they do not usually deal with time; but, even so, many critics would argue that they are concerned with narratives because human beings are story-telling animals. People will provide them with narratives when they look at them or read them, because they contain information from which it is possible to construct stories. Photographs often seem to tell us things about the people in them; shopping lists imply a great deal about people's lifestyles; and even telephone directories tell a story about people in relation to towns and addresses – a telephone directory is a structured narrative of names, families and genealogies.

In conclusion, we can say that, when approaching a piece of writing for the first time, the reader should think along at least two lines. First, it is important to consider what is specific to the text, in terms of genre, mode of publication, author, historical context, setting, stylistic devices, allusions, main theme and so on. The more thought given to these areas, the more individual portions of the narrative will seem to have significance. Second, the reader needs to pay attention to the fact that there are features all texts have in common, to do with the mechanics of language, which can be analysed profitably in any one particular piece of writing. Consideration of language in this detail is most familiar in the study of poetry, and it is likely that any analysis of a poem would take into account such aspects as imagery, repetition and metaphor, but these are also qualities of prose, so readers of fiction should pay attention to these formal features as well as to the larger issues of plot, character development, narrative style, or historical and political significance.

What is the marker looking for?

The Subject Benchmark Statement for English states that 'The assessment of students should be explicitly linked to the learning processes and outcomes of their degree programmes, which should recognise that assessment significantly influences how and what students learn.' Tutors will therefore be considering the aims and learning outcomes of the course when setting your assessment and when marking it.

It is widely acknowledged now that assessment should be formative as well as summative. This means it should help you with your future work and should be aimed at diagnosing as well as evaluating your strengths and weaknesses with regard to different elements of the assignment's tasks. As the Benchmarking Statement recognizes, if 'assessment does not provide helpful feedback that assists the student's development of their skills and knowledge, their understanding of both their own current abilities and of the ways to improve their performance, it is only fulfilling half of its function, which is to address the student as well as assess the grade'. Your best way to think about what the marker is looking for is therefore to go back to the learning outcomes of the course and think about how they relate to the assessment. The marker is often looking for evidence of your thinking more than your knowledge – the skills you have developed in argument, expression and analysis are the ones most markers will want to see demonstrated in close textual reading.

11 Assignments

English studies offers a wide variety of assessment patterns, which include familiar exercises such as examinations and assignments and, especially on creative writing modules, imaginative work. These are kept under continuous review and, on most modules, changes are made from year to year in order to provide you with a fair and practical programme of assessment. The most common form of assessment is the assignment and you may still encounter a degree where the vast majority of your pattern of assessment takes this form.

Broadly speaking, an assignment is an essay or equivalent piece of written work with a specific instruction, and students usually choose from a list of titles published with the module materials. Where examinations are designed to test a different set of skills from those required for coursework assignments and foreground factors such as memory and speed of thought, essays assess your ability to reflect at length on a given subject, research aspects to a chosen question, and formulate a convincing argument in your own time. Alternatively, as previously discussed, some modules require a presentation, which tests your awareness and reaction to an interactive situation where you need to communicate verbally, unlike the written form of the essay. Overall, however, the variety of forms of work should result in a system of assessment that aims to be fair to all, drawing on different strengths.

Essays

If you think of a degree course as a process of intellectual discovery, then essay writing forms a central part of this exploratory activity. In fact, the word *essay* means the attempt at discovering something, so lecturers will be looking for evidence in your writing that you are not merely duplicating or following material from critics, lectures, seminars and so on, but that you are attempting to argue your own viewpoint. This idea of essay writing emphasizes its central feature: *that you learn through the process of planning and writing.*

When planning your work, it is vital that you spend an appropriate amount of time attending to the thread of your own argument, and not merely flitting from point to point, or from one set of borrowed critical thoughts to another. It may be helpful not only to make a plan of the structure and key points of your essay but also a first draft which you then consider carefully, asking yourself such questions as:

- Do I provide a clear response to the question?
- Does the beginning of my essay link up with the conclusion in terms of the development of my ideas?
- Am I building the essay up through the use of quotations, or are the quotations elements which pad out what remain loosely connected points?
- How is my essay organized?
- Can I summarize the line of argument in a sentence?
- Does it address the assessment criteria of this specific assignment?

It is important to note that, in the study of literature, reference is made continually to the work of other commentators and critics. It is therefore desirable that you are aware of any important work in the area about which you are writing, but it is equally important not to be overwhelmed by other people's critical ideas, otherwise your essay will not perform its proper function. It may be best that you read critics after an initial attempt to sketch out an outline for your essay; then your reading will be governed by your own ideas, although they will not limit your writing.

Most new university students feel they have a fair grasp of essay writing and that this is less problematic than conducting the research and note-taking activities that accompany it in higher education. However, new students are likely to focus on narrative, facts and description rather than argument and analysis. Consequently, tutors in your first year are likely to encourage you to move away from either repeating the views of others verbatim or relying too heavily on your own opinions. Instead, they will emphasize the importance of discursive and academic debate 'pitting different interpretations against each other and assessing the different insights each produces'.[1] Essay writing is thus about balance: finding your voice within the range of critical registers and integrating critical opinion with your own perspective on a text or subject.

Dissertation

A dissertation is the longest essay you are likely to write. It is a substantial piece of work independently conceived and produced, usually at the end of your course. In the United States it is known as the Honour's Project and in the UK it is often the most important element in the calculation of your degree classification. It frequently provides an opportunity for you to study a topic of your choice over a whole academic year, developing your work under the close supervision of a member of staff.

The dissertation is considered in many English departments to be the culmination of your studies. You will be expected to use your skills of independent learning, close reading and critical analysis to develop a clear argument or 'thesis' over the course of many thousand words. It is the best opportunity also for you to engage in discussion with a tutor, in order to consolidate your material, exercise critical judgement and demonstrate awareness of the subject's scholarly conventions.

Because the dissertation is a much longer piece of work than an essay it is even more important that you plan it properly. The dissertation may be a topic of particular personal interest to you that you work on throughout your final year, for example. There are likely to be few or no formal classes and you will have to work independently. This is the closest you are likely to come to undertaking a research project, as your tutors would understand it. If you particularly enjoy the dissertation process it may be that you are well suited to continuing into postgraduate English studies.

Other assignments

The Benchmark Statement notes that other forms of assessment that may be used in English studies include:

- formal unseen examinations of various kinds and durations;
- 'take-away' examinations;
- coursework (including short and long essay requirements and reviews);
- project work (which might be collaborative);
- dissertations (which might require evidence of considerable scholarly research);
- oral assessment (including formal presentations, the management of meetings, assessment of seminar performance, etc.);
- external placement or work-based learning reports;
- tasks aimed at the development of specific skills (including IT and bibliographical exercises);
- portfolio work (including creative writing, reflective journals, essay plans, annotated bibliographies, created resources, etc.).

The most frequent types of alternative assessment are: essays written in non-exam conditions, sometimes during contact time (a 'class test'); individual or group projects; the preparation and presentation of a portfolio; student logs or even blogs recording the development of your understanding on the module; short answer tests; peer assessment; multiple-choice and/or computer-based tests; and vivas (oral exams), which are less common than in the past but may be used to assess borderline students who are on the cusp of a degree classification at the end of their course.

English studies now has a wider range of assessment because tutors realize the importance of encouraging different skills and recognizing different abilities. Twenty years ago a degree might have been assessed solely by examination. Ten years ago it might have been overwhelmingly assessed by essay. Now it is likely to be a blend of different assessments, each one designed to allow you to show how you have met the learning outcomes of the module.

What is the marker looking for?

All courses should provide you with assessment criteria so that you know on what basis your essay or other assignment will be marked.

The Benchmark Statement observes that markers in English are interested in the following elements:

- breadth and depth of subject knowledge, including relevant contextual knowledge and the demonstration of powers of textual analysis as appropriate;
- the management of discursive analysis and argument, including the awareness of alternative or contextualizing lines of argument;
- rhetorical strategies which demonstrate the convincing deployment and evaluation of evidence;
- independence of mind and originality of approach in interpretative and written practice;
- fluent and effective communication of ideas and sophistication of writing skills;
- critical acumen;
- informed engagement with scholarly debates.

Another thing the marker will be alert to is plagiarism: the unacknowledged use of material not your own. It is important, therefore, to make sure that you are aware of correct referencing systems and expectations before you embark on assignments. To avoid plagiarism you should cite your source when you quote other material or make substantial use of ideas taken from someone else's work, whether quoting verbatim, lightly paraphrasing, or referring to ideas derived from the work of another author. Plagiarism from websites is common and material from the internet, including popular study sites, must be acknowledged in your work just as paper-based sources must.[2]

In general terms, we might say that there are five requirements of a good essay:

1 It is well structured, well presented, and well written.
2 It demonstrates that you have undertaken and understood a range of relevant and supportive background reading in both the bibliography and in the body of the essay.
3 It makes sufficient reference to the text(s) under discussion, drawing on illustrations and quotations appropriately.

4   It displays an appropriate awareness of critical commentaries on the text(s) and of important contextual concerns.

5   It has a sustained, informed, and coherent level of argument throughout.

Finally, below are two versions of an introduction to an essay question at level 1 of an undergraduate degree course in English studies: the first answer is poor and inappropriately presented; the other is corrected and improved, although in no way offered as a model. The second version is simply meant to show how the first is deficient and may be developed.

Question: 'Choose a text you have read recently and explain why you think it is suitable for study in university English departments today.'

Answer 1

The book I have chosen to write about is 'Macbeth' by Shakespeare. It is a book that stays in the readers mind as it is full of life-like description and characters. The plays' main setting is Scotland. Which makes it a Celtic play. The character of 'Macbeth' is a thane who has ambitions to be the king. The realism of the play is shown in Shakespeares use of real places and characters from Scottish history.

Macbeth is encouraged to kill the king Duncan by his wife. She tells him they must 'screw their courage to the sticking place' if they are to take the throne from Duncan. The play can thus be read as a study of ambition and the modern reader can relate it to twenty first century politics or to people known in his or her life. As Jan Kott showed in his book 'Shakespeare our Contemporary', Macbeth can be studied 'as though it were about the present day' even though it was written 400 years ago. Lastly, the play can be said to be suitable for study in English department's today because it has true-to-life descriptions, relates to our contemporary experience, tells us something about human ambition, and displays Shakespeares mastery of the language.

Answer 2

For this assignment, I will offer a reading of Shakespeare's *Macbeth*. The essay will discuss the play in terms of the vividness of its poetic and political description as well as the subtle delineation of character. The main setting of the play is Scotland, and *Macbeth* is considered one of Shakespeare's 'Celtic' plays; it is worth noting that Shakespeare makes use of real places and characters from Scottish history.

Macbeth begins the play as a thane with ambitions to be king. He is encouraged to kill King Duncan by his wife, Lady Macbeth, who tells him they must screw their 'courage to the sticking place' if they are to take the throne (Act x, Sc x, l x). The play might thus be read as principally a study of ambition, and the modern reader might easily relate it to examples of political machinations in twenty-first century Western society. As Jan Kott showed in his classic study *Shakespeare: Our Contemporary, Macbeth* can be studied as though it were about power-politics in the post-industrial era even though it was written 400 years ago.[3]

I will conclude that the play can be said to be suitable for study in English departments today because it is a forceful and affecting study of power relations, still relates to contemporary experience, tells the reader something significant about the nature of human ambition, and displays Shakespeare's linguistic dexterity at its height, deepening our understanding of the possibilities of poetic expression.

12 English language[1]

English is spoken by over three hundred million people as a first language and over three hundred million more as a second; it is a world language in the sense that it is used internationally in both business and leisure. You will find that studying English at university level is both challenging and enjoyable; however, particularly as a native speaker of English, you may wonder what exactly you might learn about your own language. The following section therefore gives a brief overview of the aspects of language you will study and aims to help you become familiarized with some of the key concepts and ideas.

What we know as 'English' has undergone many changes and the history of the language is a subject commonly taught at level 1. When it was originally brought to this country by the Angles, Saxons and Jutes, in the fifth century, the language was in a form that would be unrecognizable to people today. What we now know as Anglo-Saxon or Old English remained until the twelfth century, and consisted of four dialects: Northumbrian, Mercian, Kentish and West Saxon. When the Vikings invaded they occupied the north and east of England, known as the Danelaw, and brought with them their own language, Old Norse. They were able to communicate with the Anglo-Saxons as both languages were Germanic in origin, although suffixes were omitted where the languages were different, which led to a simplification in the emergent English. Where there was no English equivalent word, such as in the cases of 'egg' and 'take', they were borrowed from Old Norse.

In 1066 the Normans invaded England, and brought with them Old Northern French. By the end of the fourteenth century many words of French origin had been adopted into English, and Norman French became the language of state, church and aristocracy. Old English was seldom written down, which meant there were marked changes to the language between 1150 and 1450. By this time a dominant language had emerged as what we now call Middle English, and became standardized around the London, Oxford and Cambridge dialect, since these places were the capital city (London superseded Winchester in this capacity in the twelfth century) and capitals of learning. Standardization became important in the eighteenth century, aided in particular by the publication of Dr Johnson's *Dictionary*. English has undergone relatively small changes since this time, although historical forces, such as the impact made by the British Empire and Commonwealth, mean the vocabulary in the UK is continually incorporating new words from other languages: curry from India, racoon from America and boomerang from Australia being just a few examples.

An overview of English along these lines is just one possibility amid the numerous areas of linguistic history likely to be covered on a degree course. There will be other approaches taken, from those that focus on regional variation, dialect, vocabulary or lexicology, to those that involve you in a deeper understanding of semantics, ethics or discourse analysis.

What modules might I take?

You will appreciate by now that a module is a short course lasting one or two semesters; successfully studying a number of modules (or units, etc.) will accumulate credits that add up to completion of level 1 of a degree course. Further modules chosen at levels 2 and 3 build up enough 'points' for you to graduate with an honour's degree. Each module has its own assessments, which have to be passed in order to gain the necessary points/credit. The number of modules taken may vary depending upon the institution where you study. Some modules are compulsory, meaning you have to take them, while others will be optional and can be chosen according to your interests.

Most universities will have compulsory introductory English language modules. Although the content of these will vary, you will be expected to become familiar with a number of areas, such as: variation in English, including dialects and register; phonetics, or language sounds; semantics, or word meaning; grammar and syntax, or sentence structure. A university will assume you are a competent user of English, so the modules will not usually be any more concerned with improving your skills in this area than modules on any other humanities degree, but be theoretical in nature. Research skills and study skills may be taught as separate modules in the first year. As part of these modules you may be assisted in learning to use computer tools for language study, such as Wordsmith and Cytor.

There will most likely be optional modules in the first year, which may include modules from both within the English language field and outside of it, in related subject areas. Some examples of optional modules may be media and language or the study of linguistic variants in British regions. Other related subjects that are popularly studied with English language at degree level on joint honour's courses are: other modern languages, such as French and German; creative writing; English literature, possibly including the way language relates to literature; and communication, including inter-cultural communication.

One of the main subjects that you might choose in combination with English language is linguistics, which is the study of language in general. If you select this option, there are often introductory modules to be taken at level 1, for example sociolinguistics, or language and society, and psycholinguistics, or language and psychology.

Whichever modules you choose, they will be broad enough to give a good grounding in key approaches to studying English language whilst helping you with decisions over module choices or specialisms for levels 2 and 3.

What will I do in lectures and seminars?

Lectures involve large groups of students listening actively to a talk on a specific syllabus-subject within a module; a lecture schedule, giving you a list of what the forthcoming lectures will concern, is normally distributed at the beginning of the semester or term. It is best to do some reading around this schedule so that you are prepared; most lecturers will also distribute a reading list with the schedule. You are not always expected to contribute when in lectures, but there may be a question and answer session at the end whereby students can pose queries to the lecturer. Lecturers often also circulate a handout with a basic outline of the lecture and its key points, detailing how it will be structured. If no such handout is given it may be necessary to take more detailed notes, but this should not be at the expense of listening to the lecturers and concentrating on what they are saying. After a lecture it is always a good idea to go through your notes and make sense of them.

Seminars are smaller groups with a tutor. Reading material will be specified in advance and you will be expected to do preparation work as well as come along with some of your own ideas related to the required reading. You will be expected to play a full part within the discussion and the tutor's role may be aimed at initiating further debate rather than giving you further information. Seminars vary in style: tutors may introduce a topic for discussion then ask you to talk about its various aspects in small groups before feeding back to the class as a whole; you may be given exercises to carry out either in pairs, groups or individually; or you may be sent to research a topic and then feed back, for example using IT software. Some notes can be taken in seminars, but they should be a record of your ideas as they occur in the discussion.

How will I be assessed?

There is a variety of assessment types for an English language degree course; these may include essays, presentations, exams and a dissertation completed in the final year of a degree course.

For an essay you will be asked to discuss an aspect, or aspects, of the module you are studying – generally these are topics that have been covered in lectures or seminars. As an example, for a module on the concepts and components of language you may be asked to answer the following question: ' "We recognize nouns, verbs, adjectives, adverbs, prepositions, etc. because of the **form** they take as well as their **distribution** and **function** in the sentence." Discuss, with examples'.[2] When you are writing an essay it is important to examine the question from several different viewpoints and therefore to target research and reading towards addressing the assignment title. Planning an essay is particularly important; you might want to use techniques such as 'spider diagrams' or 'mind maps' to 'map out' your answer. This enables you to link your ideas together, out of which an argument should emerge. Essays should be researched and planned well in advance of the deadline, as resources may not always be available immediately.

Presentations should be planned in a similar way to essays, and given the same amount of attention. While much of your English language study will be specialized, the transferable skills and confidence gained from doing presentations will prove useful in many careers after graduation. You may be asked to present on a given topic either in a group or as an individual. If it is a group presentation each person should be given equal research to do; the group should then collate this information and present the findings. Individual presentations can prove as challenging because it is your responsibility to do the research and presentation on your own. It is not advisable to read from a sheet of paper but, for example, to practise the presentation and talk around bullet points. You may also consider producing a handout with these points on them.

Exams can be intimidating, but with good revision techniques they will not prove a problem for most students. Revision and planning are essential, and this should be done well in advance of the exam. Practice questions may be available, and can assist with time management when taking the actual exam; for example a two-hour exam when answering two questions should be split equally in time, with one hour for each question. Students learn differently, so it is essential to know the learning styles that suit you best as an individual. For some, speaking into and listening to a Dictaphone may be the best way to revise, while for others doing 'spider diagrams' may be best. When taking the actual exam, think calmly, answer the questions thoroughly, and plan the answer systematically before beginning to write. An example of an exam question on an introductory concepts and components module might be: 'Describe the main morphological processes found in English, with examples.'[3] Here you need to register that the question is asking for descriptions, that these must be of the main processes, and that you should give examples. Appropriate attention to the requirements of each of these three parts to the question will determine the success of your answer.

The dissertation is a requirement at most universities in order to gain an honour's degree. It is often likened to a long essay that reflects your personal interests and is completed independently, with tutorial support. It is usually written in level 3 of a degree and it is wise to set aside a certain amount of time each week to work on the dissertation because you will be expected to complete it alongside other modules with more pressing deadlines.

What skills will I gain as an English language student?

A variety of skills are developed throughout an English language degree. Most obvious, perhaps, is the subject knowledge gained, which may include technical, sociological, historical and theoretical elements. However, there will be less obvious knowledge and skills you obtain while studying. Research skills are part of these, which might gathering include data and information, analysing data and interpreting statistics. Associated with this is report writing, which involves seeing an argument from several different viewpoints, problem solving and critical analysis. All of these contribute to the development of excellent communication skills; giving group presentations also enhances these skills, and will assist you in thinking about teamwork. In 2005 over half of English graduates (including English language graduates) entered full-time employment immediately after finishing their degrees. Most took up either administrative posts, which might include bi-lingual secretaries, or went into educational professions, such as teaching.

However, because English language is an academic degree, the career opportunities it affords are greater. Some careers such as speech therapy may relate to subject knowledge; however most careers do not, using instead the transferable skills gained on the degree. These may be as different as law, the media or public relations. Other graduates have successfully pursued careers in the police, diplomatic service, local government, marketing and advertising, and the tourism industry. As can be seen from this, opportunities are broad and provide challenging careers.

Further references

Introductory texts

Trask, R.L. (1999), *Language: The Basics*, 2nd edition (London: Routledge). This book gives a good, easy to understand, general introduction to the study of the English language. It includes chapters on grammar, meaning, variation, and children and language.

Freeborn, D. with French, P. and Langford, D. (1993), *Varieties of English: An Introduction to the Study of Language*, 2nd edition

(Basingstoke: Palgrave). A very practical guide to studying the English language. This book includes a cassette tape and lots of activities to assist students in their understanding and development of language skills.

Reference texts

Crystal, D. (2003), *The Cambridge Encyclopedia of Language*, 2nd revised edition (Cambridge: Cambridge University Press). This book is an excellent reference text for any student of English language. This new revised edition includes sections on the internet and world English. Also statistics and references, including further reading, have been updated.

The Oxford English Dictionary: http://www.oed.com
A website worth subscribing to. A comprehensive guide to the English language, including the meaning, history and pronunciation of over half a million words.

Journals

English Today: The International Review of the English Language, www. cambridge.org/journals/journal_catalogue.asp?mnemonic=eng

A scholarly journal that can be accessed online for a subscription fee. It is likely that universities will hold this journal as a hard copy. It covers all aspects of the English language, from the influence of new technologies to the history of the language.

The history of English

Bryson, B. (2002), *Mother Tongue: The English Language* (Oxford: Oxford University Press). A light-hearted and witty introduction to the history of the English language. Bill Bryson's book is a good preparatory text to read before beginning an English language degree.

Crystal, D. (2005), *The Stories of English* (London: Penguin). David Crystal has produced a brilliant overview of the history of the English language. Easy to understand, he traces not only the origins of standard English but of its dialects too.

Burchfield, R.W. and Simpson, J. (2002), *The English Language* (Oxford: Oxford University Press). This book demonstrates how complex the development of the English language is, tracing it along from the runes through to the twentieth century. It is an interesting read, and has won much critical acclaim for its breadth and depth.

Language variation
'BBC Voices' www.bbc.co.uk/voices/

An interactive website ideal for research into regional variation. This website shows the results of a survey of language in the UK conducted by journalists. Its interactive element makes it easy and enjoyable to use.

'The Speech Accent Archive' http://accent.gmu.edu

This website is ideal for research into regional accents in the USA. Non-native and native speakers of English were recorded saying the same paragraph of text. These have been transcribed, and are of use for analysis and comparison.

13 Creative writing[1]

While there are many kinds of writing you might pursue on your course, from autobiography to travel writing, creative writing generally falls into three main forms: fictional prose, poetry and plays. One of the main differences between further and higher education level work is the amount of reading expected of you, and this applies to creative writing courses as much as to other subjects, not least because most creative writing students find they need to read widely in order to become more competent writers themselves.[2] This not only includes reading other writers' work, but also literary criticism, which will provide you with ideas, stimulate thought, and serve as a basis for discussion with your peers.

Theory may seem a daunting thing to explore, but it is often part of a literary writer's methodological approach to creative writing. Theory has been a part of writing dating back to the times of Sir Philip Sidney, through to Wordsworth, Coleridge and Shelley to Virginia Woolf and T.S. Eliot at the beginning of the twentieth century.[3] In earlier centuries, what we now know as 'creative writing' was very much perceived as an expression of a writer's philosophy and personality. However, Roland Barthes's revolutionary 1968 essay 'The death of the author' challenged the authority of writers over meaning and gave primacy to the reader in the interpretation of texts. A theoretical framework for creative writing has developed within universities since this time, and it is common for academics who are also creative writers to research into areas such as aesthetics and genre theory. The development of new technologies such as the internet also promises exciting opportunities for the sharing of ideas and theories on a global scale. Overall, creative writing seems to have a positive future as a discipline within universities and increasing numbers of students find themselves engaged by what the subject has to offer.

What modules might I take?[4]

Most universities that offer creative writing as a degree have some form of introductory module to the subject in the first year of study. These modules often include a combination of discussing the work of published authors alongside intensive practical creative work. This may include poetry, plays, fiction and non-fiction. Other universities may begin with some genre-based modules. These modules will probably include the above genres; however, some less traditional university courses may include a broader definition of creative writing, encompassing such areas as: writing for television, radio and film, which may include producing a DVD; genre fiction, such as detective stories, as well as graphic novels and multimedia, or more factual writing, such as biography and travel writing.

Many creative writing degrees combine this course of study with English literature, which provides students with a grounding in genre studies and literary criticism. It also allows for the development of critical and analytical skills, as well as cultural awareness through the study of literature from a variety of periods up to the twenty-first century. This aspect of the degree is likely to involve some study of literary and cultural theory, which informs the work of most writers. Some universities also offer the opportunity to study some English language modules, as well as modules from other departments and faculties. Study-skills modules are another popular option for some universities to offer, and may be generic or more specific to creative writing. The module might include learning about the writing process, for example researching, revising, drafting and editing, as well as creative technique, which includes such skills as plotting and characterization.

The last main type of module offered is careers-linked. These are modules that aim to give you a sense of the publishing industry. Again, this occurs in two main forms: first, visiting-writers programmes and work placements; and second, the teaching of professional business aspects such as writing book proposals and proof-reading. However, the most striking aspect of creative writing in HE is the diversity of courses running across the UK. It is especially important, therefore, to choose one that reflects your interests and aspirations.

What will I do in creative writing workshops?[5]

Writing has a reputation as a solitary activity and so participation in workshops may seem an odd use of your time. However, writers have always found it useful to join together to read and comment on each other's work, and the workshop is simply a formalization of this activity.

A workshop may contain some or all of the following elements. You might be asked to examine a published author's work critically, but, from a writer's perspective. This might include composing a critical review, reflection, analysis or commentary in response to the author's work. You may also be given trigger exercises, which are designed to assist in the creation of ideas: you might, for example, be given ten minutes to write some snatches of dialogue on a given theme and then the opportunity to share your ideas with others.

To begin with, you will generally be put into smaller groups to share work and so should not feel intimidated when first attending workshops. Workshops are very useful in the sense that they give you inspiration, good-quality honest feedback on your work-in-progress, time to experiment with different ways of writing, and the motivation to maintain your commitment as well as enthusiasm.

How will I be assessed?[6]

Assessment for creative writing comes in two main forms: original practical work and reflective essay writing. The practical work is almost self-explanatory in that you will be expected to produce examples of your own creative writing for assessment; this may be a set of verses for a poetry-writing module, for example. Here you are expected to demonstrate engagement with a chosen genre through your writing, as well as an awareness of the work of other published writers in the same genre.

The less obvious form of assessment, which you may not have previously encountered, is reflective essay writing. The central point of these assignments is to discover something new about the practical work you are engaged in, usually through a consideration of your writing techniques in the light of primary and secondary reading. As with all essays, you are expected to form an argument and structure the essay around it. The use of critical material to support a view is welcomed, but must not become the main thread of the piece and should be read after outlining your own ideas for the essay. Writing in this way may seem intimidating, but it is necessary to acquire a range of skills in order to become a reflective creative writer.

What skills will I gain as a creative writing student?[7]

As a creative writing student it is important to understand the types of skills you will gain on the degree in order to plan for your graduate career. Creative writing develops a number of skills, most of which are transferable.

The main transferable skills are those relating to communication: both oral and written. As a creative writing student you will learn how to express ideas in a variety of different genres, and as a graduate you will be expected to have the ability to summarize, argue and debate in a variety of contexts, for example through your experiences in workshop situations and writing essays. You should find that you grow in confidence through presenting your own work to peers, developing opinions, ideas and theories as well as learning to be persuasive by using supporting evidence appropriately.

Time management is another important transferable skill. You will be required to work to strict deadlines and be highly self-motivated. Awareness of the importance of time constraints is developed by both the production of your own written work and having to read widely in a relatively short space of time. Critical skills, including the ability to be able to interpret, evaluate and assess sources, are also useful in terms of postgraduate careers. You will develop these in several different contexts: in terms of your own pieces of written work, those of peers and those of published writers. Above all, and perhaps most importantly, is the amount of valuable specialist knowledge acquired on the degree, as well as the development of your ability to be creative in both thought and action.

What type of career will a creative writing degree equip me for?

The transferable skills gained on a creative writing degree make it useful in a variety of careers, from teaching through journalism to public relations, and from arts administration to publishing, advertising or the media. However, perhaps the most obvious career paths to choose are those of writer or critic.[8] Writing is a challenging career to enter since writers are generally not 'employed' in the conventional sense of the word. If you are interested in following this career path you should consider some form of postgraduate study to develop your skills and creativity further. There is some funding available for this through the Arts and Humanities Research Council and various charitable organizations, but there is strong competition for these awards, so ensure that you contact the university's careers service and work with current lecturers on applications. Alternatively, attending a local group where peer reviews occur is also useful for developing your skills and making contacts. You will also have to be prepared to sell your work, whether this is to agents, publishers or the media, and careful consideration needs to be taken to ensure the format is appropriate. More information regarding this can be found, for example, on the BBC website (www.bbc.co.uk), alongside details of opportunities for you to apply for work-experience with the Corporation.

Allied to writing creatively is the work of a critic or reviewer. You will understand some of what this career involves already, through your reflective essay writing on the degree course. Critics generally work for either newspapers, magazines, websites or, less commonly, television, and are frequently responsible for reviewing all genres within the arts. This also includes not only carrying out relevant research on a piece of writing/performance or on a writer but also interviewing relevant participants, for example actors or the director of a theatre production. Getting involved in the student media while at university is a sound way of beginning to learn about this kind of career. There are many other possibilities, however, and as you can appreciate from the above discussion, a creative writing degree provides a solid foundation for many satisfying jobs. As more and more graduates are finding, learning the art of writing imaginatively is an excellent platform for launching a future career.

Further references section

General creative writing guides

Julia Casterton (1998), *Creative Writing: A Practical Guide*, 2nd edn (Basingstoke: Macmillan). This book gives concise, supportive advice on creative writing. It specifically examines techniques such as characterization, as well as the range of genres, including the short story and poetry.

Robert Graham, Helen Newell, Heather Leach and John Singleton (eds) (2005), *The Road to Somewhere: A Creative Writing Companion* (Basingstoke: Palgrave Macmillan). A collection of essays exploring writing in its traditional forms, as well as more experimental genres. There are exercises and examples to stimulate writing, and more theoretical essays to encourage debate and discussion.

Paul Mills (2006), *The Routledge Creative Writing Coursebook* (London: Routledge). This is a very practical guide to creative writing in all its forms. It may be particularly useful if you have never done any creative writing before. The chapters are genre based and include children's fiction, film, radio and theatre.

Julia Bell (ed.) (2001), *The Creative Writing Coursebook* (London: Pan). This book is perhaps the most well known of its kind, since it was inspired by the first creative writing university course, at the University of East Anglia. It includes contributions by such writers as Malcolm Bradbury, Andrew Motion and Ali Smith. The book itself guides the beginner through all stages of the writing process, with practical exercises, to the point of becoming published.

The novel

John Gardner (1999), *On Becoming a Novelist* (London: W.W. Norton). Described as inspirational, this book is not a step-by-step guide to becoming a novelist in a conventional manner. It does not contain practical exercises; instead its main aim is to explore what it means to be a novelist.

Poetry

Robin Behn (1992), *Practice of Poetry: The Writing Exercises from Poets who Teach* (London: HarperCollins). This is a very practical guide to writing poetry. It is suitable for use on your own or, alternatively, for discussion in poetry workshops.

Plays
Noel Greig (2005), *Playwriting: A Practical Guide* (London: Routledge). Greig's book is a comprehensive guide to writing for the theatre. It contains a wealth of practical exercises, from building characters to writing multiple drafts.

Philosophy of creative writing
Nigel Krauth and Tess Brady (eds) (2006), *Creative Writing: Theory Beyond Practice* (Teneriffe: Post Pressed, 2006). This collection of essays brings together writers, teachers and theorists who examine the underlying philosophy behind creative writing from perspectives as broad as architecture and ecology.

Creative writing websites
'100 Words' www.100words.net

This website began in 2001 and has grown in popularity. One hundred words of text every day for a month is the commitment you must make. This is a particularly good exercise when embarking on a degree because it instils self-discipline and creativity: core skills needed on a creative writing degree.

'Association for Creative Writing and English'
www.hlss.mmu.ac.uk/english/acwe/

This free website gives information on workshops, reading events, and publishing and competition opportunities. Perhaps of most interest is that the site provides access to creative writing journals, which will be useful when writing critical assignments.[9]

Notes

Part One

1 See UKstudentlife: http://www.ukstudentlife.com/index.htm
2 Siobhán Holland, *Access and Widening Participation: A Good Practice Guide*, English Subject Centre Report Series, 4, February 2003, p. 16.

Chapter 1

1 Source: 'A review of black and minority ethnic participation in higher education',
   www.aimhigher.ac.uk/sites/practitioner/resources/
   Conf%20Summary%20report%20final%20(2).pdf
2 See   www.english.heacademy.ac.uk/archive/publications/reports/
   curr_teach_main.pdf, English Subject Centre, 'Survey of the English curriculum and teaching in UK higher education', Report Series, Number 8, October 2003.

Chapter 2

1 See   www.english.heacademy.ac.uk/archive/publications/reports/
   curr_teach_main.pdf, English Subject Centre, 'Survey of the English curriculum and teaching in UK higher education', Report Series, Number 8, October 2003.
2 Holland, S. (2003), 'Access and widening participation: a good practice guide', English Subject Centre Report Series, Number 4, February, p. 6.
3 See the Introduction to Eagleton, T. (1983), *Literary Theory* (Oxford: Blackwell).

Chapter 3

1 Help in writing and researching this chapter was given by Claire Philpott.

2   See   www.english.heacademy.ac.uk/archive/publications/reports/
    curr_teach_main.pdf, English Subject Centre, 'Survey of the English
    curriculum and teaching in UK higher education', Report Series,
    Number 8, October 2003.

Chapter 4

1   Information here has been adapted from *The Value of Higher Education*
    by Vikki Pickering,
    www.cihe-uk.com/docs/PUBS/0503ValueHEStudents.pdf
2   This section was drafted by Claire Philpott.
3   Martin, P. and Gawthrope, J. (2004), 'The study of English and the
    careers of its graduates', in Knight, P. and Yorke, M. (eds) *Learning,
    Curriculum and Employability in Higher Education* (London: Routledge)
    p. 74.
4   Appleton, Diane (2004), *Your Degree in English . . . What Next?*
    Liverpool: AgCAS, February. pp. 1–2.
5   The Teacher Training Agency, *Experience Teaching*,
    www.tda.gov.uk/Recruit/experienceteaching.aspx
6   The Teacher Training Agency, *Life as a Teacher*,
    www.tda.gov.uk/Recruit/lifeasateacher.aspx
7   Kingston, Paul, *Occupational Profile: Commissioning Editor*,
    www.prospects.ac.uk/downloads/occprofiles/profile_pdfs/
    Y1_Commissioning_editor.pdf
8   Zajac, Camilla, *Occupational Profile: Publishing Copy-editor/Proofreader*,
    www.prospects.ac.uk/downloads/occprofiles/profile_pdfs/
    Y1_Publishing_copy-editor_proofreader.pdf
9   Proudfoot, Rachel, *Occupational Profile: Bookseller*,
    www.prospects.ac.uk/downloads/occprofiles/profile_pdfs/
    H3_Bookseller.pdf, p. 2.
10 Whatnall, David, *Occupational Profile: Academic Librarian*,
    www.prospects.ac.uk/downloads/occprofiles/profile_pdfs/
    W1_Academic_librarian.pdf
11 Thompson, Rhoma. Occupational Profile: Public Librarian
    http://www.prospects.ac.uk/downloads/occprofiles/profile_pdfs/
    W1_Public_librarian.pdf Accessed 11/10/07.
12 Kay, June, *Occupational Profile: Broadcasting Journalist*,
    www.prospects.ac.uk/downloads/occprofiles/profile_pdfs/
    Y2_Broadcasting_journalist.pdf
13 Dawson, Hilary, *Occupational Profile: Newspaper Journalist*,
    www.prospects.ac.uk/downloads/occprofiles/profile_pdfs/
    Y2_Newspaper_journalist.pdf

14 Trickey, Graham (2004) 'The Call of the Bar' in Trickey, Graham (ed.) *Prospects: Law 2004/05*. Manchester: Graduate Prospects, pp. 168–169.

15 The Law Careers Advice Network, *The Non-law Degree Route – Solicitors*, www.lcan.org.uk/qualifying/the_non_law_degree_route.htm

16 Graduate Prospects Ltd and AgCAS, *English – 2003 Graduates*, www.prospects.ac.uk/cms/ShowPage/Home_page//What_do_ graduates_do_2005/charts_and_tables_pages/p!eiglkfk?subject_id=12

17 See Martin and Gawthrope [3].

18 Martin and Gawthrope [3], p. 74.

19 University of Gloucestershire Careers Centre (2004) *Careers Centre: Support for Students, Staff and Graduates of the University*. Cheltenham: Careers Centre, pp. 1–2.

20 'The good, the bad and the tea-making' in Shanahan, Andrew (ed), *Prospects Work Experience 2004/5*. Manchester: Prospects Ltd, p 6.

21 Prospects, *Voluntary Work*, www.prospects.ac.uk/cms/ShowPage/Home_page/Explore_types_ of_jobs/Types_of_Job/p!eipaL?state=showocc&idno=53

22 See Martin and Gawthrope [3].

23 This can be found on the Prospects website under 'What jobs would suit me?' – in the 'Jobs and work section'. You will need to register with an email address but the registration is free, www.prospects.ac.uk/cms/ShowPage/Home_page/ What_jobs_would_suit_me___Prospects_Planner_/Show_login_ page/p!eLaXgjk

24 Fazackerley, Anna, *Students want to stay on*, www.timeshighereducation.co.uk/story.asp?storyCode=177554& sectioncode=26, p. 1.

25 Ewing, Jim (General Secretary of the Postgraduate Committee) quoted in 'What the experts say' in O'Connor, Joanne (ed.) (2005) *Prospects Postgrad 2005/6*. Manchester: Graduate Prospects Ltd, p. 6.

Part Two

1 For example, see the EPPI-centre review of personal development planning effectiveness at: http://eppi.ioe.ac.uk/EPPIWebContent/reel/review_groups/EPPI/ LTSN/LTSN_June03.pdf

2 Timms, Jane (2003), *Making Applications*. Sheffield: AgCAS, p. 5.

3 For a full report, involving a second wave of interviews, see: www.unite-group.co.uk/data/Reports/The%20Student% 20Living%20Report%202002.pdf

Chapter 5

1   Smith, L. (2004), 'An investigation into the experience of first-year students of English at British universities', *Arts & Humanities in Higher Education* vol. 3(1), 81–93.
2   See www.english.ltsn.ac.uk, English Subject Centre, *Survey of the English Curriculum and Teaching in UK Higher Education*, Report Series, Number 8, October 2003.
3   Advice here and in some other parts of this book is partly drawn from the University of Gloucestershire's handbook for students studying English.

Chapter 6

1   Help in writing and researching this chapter was given by Claire Philpott.
2   Boolean syntax makes use of operators such as AND and OR. For a useful explanation see www.brightplanet.com/resources/deails/tutorial–part–4.html
3   A useful discussion on this topic will be found in Hawthorn, J., Goring, P. and Mitchell, D. (2001), *Studying Literature: The Essential Companion* (London: Arnold).

Chapter 7

1   Examples in this section were devised by Peter Widdowson.

Chapter 8

1   See Smith, K. (2004), 'An investigation into the experience of first-year students of English at British universities', *Arts & Humanities in Higher Education*, vol. 3(1), 81–93.
2   These are the processes recommended by Derek Rowntree in his well-established book *Learn How to Study* (2002) (New York: TimeWarner).
3   For a discussion of each of these see the 'Introduction' to Cottrel, S. (2006), *The Exam Skills Handbook* (Oxford: Macmillan).

Chapter 9

1   Keverne Smith says in 'An investigation into the experience of first-year students of English at British universities', *Arts & Humanities in*

Higher Education 2004, vol. 3(1), 81–93): 'Of the remaining 17 per cent, 9 per cent thought lectures the most valuable method, 5 per cent one-to-one tutorials, and 3 per cent workshops.'
2   Several of these tips have been adapted from a resource providing support for formal presentation speaking and oral communication created by Patricia Palmerton. For further details see the full website: www.hamline.edu/personal/ppalmerton/ocxc_site/Welcome.htm

Chapter 11

1   Keverne Smith (2004), 'An investigation into the experience of first-year students of English at British universities', *Arts & Humanities in Higher Education 2004*, vol. 3(1), 81–93.
2   For example, material in this section is derived from the University of Gloucestershire's (2003), *Handbooks for Students Studying English Literature, English Language and Creative Writing*, originally prepared by Dr Deborah Thacker (Cheltenham: University of Gloucestershire).
3   Kott, J. (1964), *Shakespeare Our Contemporary* (London: Methuen).

Chapter 12

1   This chapter was originally researched and drafted by Claire Philpott.
2   Specimen essay question taken from the University of Gloucestershire first year undergraduate English language degree module 'EZ103: What is language? Concepts and components' November 2006. Module tutor: Dr Jonathan Marshall.
3   Specimen exam question. *Ibid.*

Chapter 13

1   This chapter was originally researched and drafted by Claire Philpott.
2   Information for this paragraph is based on McLoughlin, N. (2006), *Creative Writing: Field Guide 2006–2007* (Cheltenham: University of Gloucestershire) p. 10.
3   Information for this paragraph is based on Brady, T. and Krauth, N. (2006), 'Towards creative writing theory' in Krauth, N. and Brady, T. (eds) *Creative Writing: Theory Beyond Practice* (Teneriffe: Post Pressed) pp. 13–18.
4   Information for this section comes from an internet search and survey of 20 UK universities conducted by the author.
5   Information for this section is based on Heather Leach (2004), 'Writing together: groups and workshops' in Graham, R., Leach, H.,

Newell, H. and Singleton, J. (eds) *The Road to Somewhere: A Creative Writing Companion* (Basingstoke: Palgrave Macmillan) pp. 89–100. Also thanks go to Tiffany Murray for enabling the author to watch a creative writing workshop for WT102: prose fundamentals, at the University of Gloucestershire, on 30 April 2007.

6   Information for this paragraph is based on McLoughlin, N. (2006), *Field of Creative Writing: Field Guide 2006–2007* (Cheltenham: University of Gloucestershire) pp. 17–21. Also used was '15: assessment criteria' in Murray, T. (2007) *WT102: Prose Fundamentals: Syllabus* (Cheltenham: University of Gloucestershire) p. 11.

7   Information for this paragraph is based on McLoughlin, N. (2006), *Field of Creative Writing: Field Guide 2006–2007* (Cheltenham: University of Gloucestershire) pp. 41–42.

8   Information for the following two paragraphs is based on 'Writer' and 'Critic'
www.prospects.ac.uk/links/occupations

9   Thanks go to Tiffany Murray and Nigel McLoughlin for their assistance with this section.

Further reading and resources

Here you will find many references to paper-based and on-line resources that will help you with your degree in English studies. Additionally, to find out statistical data about student experiences of universities in the UK, I strongly recommend you go to: www.unistats.com/

Five key resources you should have

1 A good dictionary, e.g. the *Concise Oxford* (UK) or *Webster's* (USA).
2 A good thesaurus, e.g. *Roget's Thesaurus*, published by Penguin.
3 A dictionary of literary terms, e.g. Childs, P. and Fowler, R. (eds) (2006), *The Routledge Dictionary of Literary Terms* (London: Routledge).
4 A guide to the pitfalls and niceties of using language, such as the widely available Fowler's Modern English Usage (Oxford: Oxford University Press).
5 An overview of literary history and chronology such as Widdowson, P. (2004), *The Palgrave Guide to English Literature and its Contexts* (Basingstoke: Palgrave); or Cox, M. (2004), *The Concise Oxford Chronology of English Literature* (Oxford: Oxford University Press).

To help with reading and thinking

Buzan, T. (1989), *Use Your Head*, revised edn (London: BBC Books).
Buzan, T. (1995), *The Mind Map Book*, 3rd.edn (London: BBC Books).

Cottrell, S. (2003), *The Study Skills Handbook*, 2nd edn (Basingstoke: Palgrave).

Drew, S. and Bingham, R. (1997), *The Student Skills Guide* (Aldershot: Gower).

Payne, E. and Whittaker, L. (2000), *Developing Essential Study Skills* (Harlow: Financial Times/Prentice Hall).

Race, P. (1992), *500 Tips for Students* (Oxford: Blackwell).

Smith, M. and Smith, G. (1990), *A Study Skills Handbook* (Oxford: Oxford University Press).

To help with writing

Barnes, R. (1995), *Successful Study for Degrees* (London: Routledge).

Barrass, R. (1982), *Students Must Write: A Guide to Better Writing in Course Work and Examinations* (London: Routledge).

Berry, R. (1995), *The Research Project: How to Write It* (London: Routledge).

Blight, G. (1996), *Mastering English Spelling* (Basingstoke: Macmillan).

Burton, S.H. (1984), *Mastering English Grammar* (Basingstoke: Macmillan).

Burton, S.H. and Humphries, J.A. (1996), *Mastering English Language* (Basingstoke: Macmillan).

Casey, F. (1993), *How to Study: A Practical Guide* (Basingstoke: Macmillan).

Collinson, D., Kirkup, G., Kyd, R. and Slocombe, L. (1992), *Plain English*, 2nd edn (Buckingham: Open University Press).

Cottrell, S. (2005), *Critical Thinking Skills* (Basingstoke: Palgrave).

Fairbairn, G.J. and Winch, C. (1996), *Reading, Writing and Reasoning: A Guide for Students*, 2nd edn (Buckingham: Open University Press).

Greetham, B. (2001), *How to Write Better Essays* (Basingstoke: Palgrave).

Northedge, A. (1990), *The Good Study Guide* (Buckingham: Open University Press).

Peck, J. and Coyle, M. (2005), *Write it Right* (Basingstoke: Palgrave).

Pirie, D.B. (1985), *How to Write Critical Essays: A Guide for Students of Literature* (London: Routledge).

Theory, terms and concepts

It is worthwhile obtaining a guide to literary theory as well as one that covers terms more generally. The best available is probably still:

Hawthorn, J. (2001), *A Glossary of Contemporary Literary Theory*, 4th edn (London: Arnold).

Literary theory links

Glossary of Literary Theory at the University of Toronto English Library www.library.utoronto.ca/utel/glossary/headerindex.html

Literary terms and concepts

A useful online guide by John Lye at Brock University with many links to other relevant sites can be found at www.brocku.ca/english/courses/4F70/

VirtualSalt: A Glossary of Literary Terms by Robert Harris www.virtualsalt.com/litterms.htm
The Cambridge English Faculty Virtual Classroom Glossary of Literary Terms www.english.cam.ac.uk/vclass/terms.htm
Bob's Byway: a glossary of poetic terms by Robert G. Shubinski www.poeticbyway.com/glossary.html

Complete literary texts online

Use the following links to access different databases containing online literary texts.

Full Text Great Literature Classics – A Teaching and educational website from the Book Worm organization www.book-worm.org/index.htm
The Online Literature Library – the full and unabridged texts of classic works of English literature, and of classic scientific texts http://www.literature.org
Project Gutenberg – the internet's oldest producer of free electronic books http://promo.net/pg/
The Electronic Text Center from the University of Virginia Library http://etext.lib.virginia.edu/collections/languages/english/

The Oxford Text Archive from the University of Oxford http://
ota.ahds.ac.uk/

General skills

Clarke, A. (2005), *IT Skills for Successful Study* (Basingstoke: Palgrave).

Cottrell, S. (2003), *Skills for Success* (Basingstoke: Palgrave).

Cottrell, S. (2006), *The Exam Skills Handbook* (Basingstoke: Palgrave).

Littleford, D., Halstead, J. and Mulraine, C. (2004), *Career Skills* (Basingstoke: Palgrave).

van Emden, J. and Becker, L. (2003), *Effective Communication for Arts and Humanities Students* (Basingstoke: Palgrave).

van Emden, J. and Becker, L. (2004), *Presentation Skills for Students* (Basingstoke: Palgrave).

Language

Additional resources to those mentioned in Chapter 12 are:

Carter, R. (2001), *Working with Texts*, 2nd edn (London: Routledge).

Fromkin, V., Rodman, R. and Hyams, N. (2002), *An Introduction to Language*, 7th edn (London: Heinle & Heinle).

Yule, G. (2005), *The Study of Language*, 3rd edn (Cambridge: Cambridge University Press).

Creative writing

Additional resources to those mentioned in Chapter 13 are:

Anderson, L. (2005), *Creative Writing: A Workbook with Readings* (London: Routledge).

Braine, J. (1974), *Writing a Novel* (London: Methuen).

Browne, R. and King, D. (1994), *Self-Editing for Fiction Writers* (New York: HarperCollins).

McKee, R. (1999), *Story Structure* (London: Methuen).

Mills, P. (1996), *Writing in Action* (London: Routledge).

Queneau, R. (1998), *Exercises in Style* (London: Calder Publications).

Singleton, J. and Luckhurst, M. (eds) (1996), *The Creative Writing Handbook: Techniques for New Writers* (Basingstoke: Macmillan).

English literary study

Cuddon, J.A. (1999), *The Penguin Dictionary of Literary Terms and Literary Theory* (Harmondsworth: Penguin).

Fabb, N. and Durant, A. (1993), *How to Write Essays, Dissertations and Theses in Literary Studies* (Harlow: Longman).

Hawthorn, J. (2001), *Studying Literature: The Essential Companion* (Arnold).

Hawthorn, J. (2001), *Studying the Novel* (London: Arnold).

Lennard, J. (1996), *The Poetry Handbook: A Guide to Reading Poetry for Pleasure and Practical Criticism* (Oxford: Oxford University Press).

Matterson, S. and Jones, D. (2000), *Studying Poetry* (London: Arnold).

Wallis, M. (2002), *Studying Plays* (London: Arnold).

Literature websites

http://andromeda.rutgers.edu/~jlynch/Terms/

A very comprehensive (century by century) list of links to literary websites.

http://crossroads.georgetown.edu/

Resources for students interested in North American literature.

www.ctheory.com/ctheory.html_Theory discussion site.

Critical essays, etc.

http://extra.shu.ac.uk/emls/emlshome.html

Journal for students and researchers in the area of early modern literature.

www.lib.ncsu.edu/stacks/alex-index.html

A vast virtual library, with thousands of texts.

www.literature.org/

A number of texts in electronic form. Good on Gothic.

www.victoriandatabase.com

Good Victorian links.

Glossary: the language of HE and the language of literature

The language of HE

AHRC – Arts and Humanities Research Council.

Contact-time – Timetabled interaction between lecturers and students.

Course (of study) – The award for which you are studying, e.g. English language, or English literature and Creative Writing. Also called 'programme'.

CSU – Careers Service Unit.

Curriculum – The overall course of study, e.g. the English curriculum.

DfES – Department for Education and Skills.

DipHE – Diploma in Higher Education.

Dissertation – It is common for honour's degree programmes to include a large independent study module or unit called the 'dissertation' or 'project', especially in the final year. It is often thought to be the culmination of the degree.

English 'Subject Benchmark Statement' – An overview of the characteristics of English degree level study (to see the statement go to: www.qaa.ac.uk/academicinfrastructure/benchmark/honours/english.asp).

English Subject Centre – one of the Higher Education Academy's many disciplinary centres aiming to encourage and support good practice in teaching and learning: see www.english.heacademy.ac.uk/

HE – Higher education.

HEA – Higher Education Academy: a national government-funded body that works with institutions, discipline groups and individual staff to provide the best possible learning experience for all students.

HEFC – Higher Education Funding Council.

HEIs – Higher education institutions: universities and HE colleges.

HERO – Higher Education and Research Opportunities in the United Kingdom; the official gateway to HEIs.

HNDs – Higher National Diplomas.

LEA – Local Education Authority.

Lecture – A scheduled talk of usually 40+ minutes.

LSC – Learning Skills Council.

Module – The individual unit of study taken on the course.

National Student Survey – According to Hefce: 'The aim of the National Student Survey (NSS) is to gather feedback on the quality of students' courses, to help inform the choices of future applicants to higher education, and to contribute to public accountability.' See www.thestudentsurvey.com/

'New' university sector – Refers to HE-sector colleges and to universities brought into existence by or since the government act of 1992 which allowed polytechnics to apply to take the title 'university'.

NUS – National Union of Students. See www.nusonline.co.uk/

OFFA – Office for Fair Access introduced by the 2004 Higher Education Act that aimed to widen access to HE beyond traditional groups and introduced variable tuition fees.

'Old' university sector – This loose term refers to universities in existence prior to 1992.

QAA – Quality Assurance Agency for Higher Education: the body responsible for ensuring standards in HEIs are monitored and enhanced.

Reading – A specialist term in English studies that means something a little different (depending on context) from its lay use; to 'read' is to analyse and critique.

Semester – Most universities these days have semesters along USA lines, with one starting in September and one in February (cf. Term).

Seminar – Scheduled classroom contact-time between a tutor and a group of students.

SENDA – Special Educational Needs and Disability Act 2001.

SLC – Student Loans Company.

Syllabus – Books or topics to be studied in the course.

Term – Traditionally universities have three terms, separated by Christmas, Easter and the summer recess (cf. Semester).

Tutorial – One student or a small group of students scheduled to discuss a topic or text with a tutor, most commonly on a dissertation/project module or independent study module.

UCAS – Universities and Colleges Admissions Service.

Units – See Modules.

The language of literature

Allusion – An overt or indirect reference to something else, whether a text, person, event or anything else.

Alliteration – Repeated rhyming consonant sounds.

Assonance – Repeated rhyming vowel sounds.

Ballad – A poem, composed for singing, that narrates a story, usually dramatic. A traditional ballad, passed down from generation to generation by word of mouth, typically has a simple verse structure, refrains, stock phrases, repetitions, dialogue and an impersonal narrator. A literary ballad is a work written in imitation of the traditional ballad.

Bildungsroman – A German word that translates as 'novel of development'. It is associated with novels that show an individual coming of age or serving some kind of apprenticeship. Its main theme is therefore usually the protagonist's growth or development from childhood to adulthood. Examples are Dickens's *David Copperfield*, Twain's *Huckleberry Finn*, and Charlotte Brontë's *Jane Eyre*.

Ellipsis – A gap in the text usually indicated by three dots, which are called an ellipsis. An ellipsis requires the reader either to reconcile themselves to the omission, and conjecture on its importance, or to speculate on what has been repressed: what has gone unsaid or un-narrated.

Figure of speech – An unusual use of language, usually non-literal and usually to associate or compare unconnected things. The best known figures of speech are metaphor, metonymy, personification, simile and synecdoche.

Free indirect discourse – The representation of speech or thoughts without tags (such as 'he said' or 'she thought') or quotation marks.

Genre – The three major genres of literature are poetry, prose fiction and drama, but there are many subgenres such as gothic, satire, tragedy, comedy, the *Bildungsroman*, the picaresque, the ode or the sonnet.

Gothic – The Gothic novel is a subgenre of fiction usually considered to have been initiated by Horace Walpole's *The Castle of Otranto* (1764). Some of the subgenre's characteristics include a gloomy setting, dark mysteries, an atmosphere of foreboding, simplistically good or evil characters, passionate natures, remote locations and graphic or implied horror. Its heyday continued until the 1820s, but novels and films in the Gothic mode still appear regularly. Mary Shelley's *Frankenstein* is in the Gothic vein, and Angela Carter's 'The Bloody Chamber' is in part a pastiche of it.

Intertextuality – Although often employed as a synonym for allusion, reference or echo, intertextuality refers to the belief that all texts are made up of citations and are weaves of other texts.

Irony – A term in rhetoric to signal a gap between word and meaning, between what is said and what is meant or conveyed.

Linear plot – A plot that proceeds chronologically, without extended flashbacks or significant atemporal ordering of events in the narrative.

Metafiction – In Patricia Waugh's words, this is 'fiction which calls attention to itself as an artifact in order to raise questions about the relationship between fiction and reality'.

Metaphor and metonymy – Figures of speech. Metaphor works by substituting one word or image for another in terms of resemblance. By contrast, metonymy works by contiguity and association, and replaces an object with its attribute (e.g. 'the deep' instead of 'the sea'). Metonymy is often considered also to include synecdoche, which replaces the part for the whole ('hands' for 'workers') or the whole for the part ('Scotland played hockey last night').

Mimesis and diegesis – Mimesis is a word used by Plato in *The Republic* to describe the imitative representation of speech. By contrast, diegesis is the term he uses to indicate when 'the poet himself is the speaker and does not even attempt to suggest to us that anyone but himself is speaking'. In narrative, diegesis is distinguished from mimesis to describe the way narrators indirectly report and summarize speech or scenes (telling) rather than presenting them directly through monologue, dialogue or direct speech (showing). Aristotle, in his *Poetics*, expands mimesis to include the 'imitation of an action' as well as the representation of speech.

Modernism – The vast majority of attempts to offer alternative modes of representation to *realism*, from the middle of the nineteenth century to the middle of the twentieth century, have at one time or another been termed Modernist, and this applies to literature, music, painting, film and architecture (and to some works before and after this period). In poetry, Modernism is associated with moves to break from the iambic pentameter as the basic unit of verse, to introduce *vers libre*, symbolism and other new forms of writing. In prose, Modernism is associated with attempts to render human subjectivity in ways more real than realism: to represent consciousness, perception, emotion, meaning and the individual's relation to society through, among other tools, interior monologue, stream of consciousness, defamiliarization, rhythm and irresolution. Modernist writers therefore struggled, in Ezra Pound's brief phrase, to 'make it new', to modify if not overturn existing modes of representation, partly by pushing them towards the abstract or the introspective, and to express the new sensibilities of their time: in a compressed, condensed, complex literature of the city, of industry and technology, war, machinery and speed, mass markets and communication, of internationalism, the New Woman, the aesthete, the nihilist and the flâneur.

Oedipus/Electra complex – According to Freud, a number of largely unconscious feelings in the under-five child focusing on the wish to possess the parent of the opposite sex and overthrow the parent of the same sex.

Pathetic fallacy – An expression coined by John Ruskin in 1856 in *Modern Painters* to describe the way inanimate nature may be endowed with human emotions in art (one of Ruskin's examples is Kingsley's 'cruel, crawling foam' in *Alton Locke*). Another would be Forster's line in the opening of *A Passage to India*: 'when the sky chooses, glory can rain into the Chandrapore bazaars'.

Personification – A figure of speech in which something non-human is treated in human terms.

Picaresque – From the Spanish *picaro*, an unpleasant anti-social character of low birth in sixteenth-century novels. In English literature picaresque has come to mean a rambling, episodic story with a narrator or hero from the lower classes. Novels discussed in terms of this subgenre are: Defoe's *Moll Flanders*, Fielding's *Tom Jones* and Dickens's *Nicholas Nickleby*.

Prolepsis – A figure of speech in which a future event is treated as though it has happened or is happening.

Readerly and writerly – Terms coined by Roland Barthes in his book *S/Z* to distinguish the way 'classic realist' texts can encourage their passive consumption by conforming to familiar narrative codes (e.g. of coherence, linear structure, clear plot, strong characterization and historical specificity) and experimental texts which disrupt those codes and so place a greater weight on the reader's active participation in the construction of the text's meanings.

Realism – Realism, according to many critics, is characterized by its attempt objectively to offer up a mirror to the world, thus disavowing its own culturally conditioned processes and ideological stylistic assumptions. Realism, modelled on prose forms such as history and journalism, generally features characters, language, and a spatial and temporal setting very familiar to its contemporary readers, and often presents itself as transparently representative of the author's society. The hegemony of realism was challenged by Modernism and then postmodernism, as alternative ways of representing reality and the world. Realism itself was once a new, innovative form of writing, with authors such as Daniel Defoe (1660–1731) and Samuel Richardson (1690–1761) providing a different template for fiction from the previously dominant mode of prose writing, the Romance, which was parodied in one of the very first novels, Cervantes' *Don Quixote* (1605–1615), and survives in Gothic and fantasy fiction. Throughout modern literary history, realism remains the favourite style of writing for novelists. 'Classic realism', which flowered in the nineteenth century, has been delineated by critics such as Roland Barthes, Colin MacCabe and Catherine Belsey. It is a term used to describe the work of such writers as Balzac, Dickens, Mrs Gaskell and George Eliot: novels with reliable narrators who deal with contemporary social and political problems. David Lodge provides this summary in **After Bakhtin** (London: Routledge, 1990: 26): 'The mode of classic realism with its concern for coherence and causality in narrative structure, for the autonomy of the individual self in the presentation of character, for a readable homogeneity and urbanity of style, is equated with liberal humanism, with empiricism, common sense and the presentation of bourgeois culture as a kind of nature.'

Romance – Romance has its origin in medieval literature. First used to describe verse narratives about knights and heroes – the best known example is *Sir Gawain and the Green Knight*, which dates from 1375. From the latter part of the eighteenth century, a romance is a story in which the scenes and incidents are surrounded by an atmosphere of strangeness and mystery. The Romance involves heroes, the supernatural, symbols, and adventure. Romance aims at the embodiment of psychic or moral truths which cannot be expressed through a depiction of everyday reality. It is therefore concerned with unreal or fantastic worlds in order to deal with the beliefs, principles and ethical systems that lay behind human behaviour but which are not necessarily evident if we simply observe what people do.

Signifier/signified – For the Swiss linguist, Ferdinand de Saussure, the signifier and signified are the two sides to the linguistic sign, which previously had been considered to be 'a word' and 'a thing'. The signifier refers to the sound image or written mark used to represent an abstract concept or idea – the signified. For Saussure the two were inseparable despite the relation between them being arbitrary.

Spatial reading – The idea that every part of a text has to be considered in the light of the knowledge of every other part. The complex construction of many texts militates against drawing conclusions from any part of them in isolation.

Structuralism – A theoretical school heavily influenced by the linguistic study of Ferdinand de Saussure and based on the belief that all elements of culture can be understood in terms of and as parts of sign systems. For structuralists, anything that people do or use to convey information of any type is a sign. Influential European structuralists such as Roman Jakobson, Claude Lévi-Strauss and Roland Barthes attempted to develop a semiotics, or science, of signs.

Unreliable narrator – A narrator who does not properly comprehend the world and whose judgements the reader mistrusts.

Verisimilitude – The appearance or semblance of truth to nature or reality.

16 A little test: answers

	Yes or No?
1. Which of the following words are spelled correctly?	
occassion	No
committee	Yes
neccessary	No
paralell	No
parliment	No
2. Which of the following words are spelled correctly?	
cemetery	Yes
seperate	No
goverment	No
deceive	Yes
concious	No
3. Which of the following are sentences?	
About a boy.	No
You thief.	No
Loves me like a rock.	No
You exist.	Yes
The sound of silence.	No
4. In which of the following sentences are all the commas correctly placed?	
He is here, but, she is there.	No
They are going, now.	No
I am young, free and single.	Yes

No one knows, the trouble I have seen.	No
Entering the pub, I noticed her in the corner.	Yes

5. Which of these sentences make sense?

Coming round the mountain, the pub appeared in the distance.	No
Going to Mars, the astronauts would need copious supplies.	Yes
Looking out of the window, the car was at the end of the street.	No
Thinking quickly, I gave the necessary reply.	Yes
Though they were passed their sell-by date, the men ate the eggs.	No

6. Which of these sentences have an excess word?

This ever-changing world in which we live in is too fast for me.	Yes
The last thing of which I thought of was my own safety.	Yes
I want to buy a house on the street you live on.	No
The school to which she went to was far away.	Yes
Of the five remaining, two were highly thought of by the selection panel.	No

7. In which of these sentences is the semi-colon correctly used?

I am old; you are young.	Yes
There are three people in the room; Sue, John and Mary.	No
He is late; you should go.	Yes
The cat is by the door and; the dog is by the fire.	No
It is time; to go.	No

8. Which of these sentences could be considered grammatically correct?

It is hot, the sun is shining.	No
It is hot: the sun is shining.	Yes
It is hot. The sun is shining.	Yes
It is hot; the sun is shining.	Yes
It is hot and the sun is shining.	Yes

9. Which of these sentences are grammatically correct ?

We would of gone tomorrow.	No
They gave the tickets to you and I.	No
He is over their.	No
It is I.	Yes
Nobody effects me.	No

10. Which of these sentences imply that judges should not take sides?

Judges should be disinterested.	Yes
Judges should be impartial.	Yes
Judges should be uninterested.	No
Judges should be partial.	No
Judges should be unbiased.	Yes

11. In which of these sentences are the apostrophes used correctly?

It's a dog's life.	Yes
That's the dog's bone.	Yes
It's a girl.	Yes
Every dog has it's day.	No
It's raining men.	Yes

12. In which of these phrases are the apostrophes used correctly?

It's a man's bag!	Yes
The womens' movement.	No
Boys' don't cry.	No
The girls' have left.	No
The working-men's club.	Yes

Index

Learning Resources
Centre